Simple American Cooking REVISED EDITION

WILLIAMS-SONOMA

Simple **American** Cooking REVISED EDITION

Recipes by
CHUCK WILLIAMS

Photographs by
ALLAN ROSENBERG

WELDON OWEN
PUBLISHING

Contents

Introduction

Since Williams-Sonoma first opened in the 1950s, much has changed in the world of food and entertaining. Times have changed, but America—the bold, the beautiful, and the bountiful—remains a country that embraces newcomers and their cultures and cuisines. All are welcome here, and in that boundless spirit, this revised edition of *Simple American Cooking* looks back at some of the classic all-American recipes that continue to comfort and sustain as well as emphasize the importance of fresh food prepared simply and well.

Few of us have the time these days to devote to hours-long toil over a hot stove, but we all want to enjoy creating and eating dishes that are quick and easy as well as refreshingly light and delightfully healthy. On special occasions, we want our own creations to be as sophisticated and beautiful as the food we find at our favorite restaurants. *Simple American Cooking* combines the knowledge of today's realities and an appreciation for the past's pleasures.

Here you'll find recipes for uncomplicated, substantial, and heart-warming comfort foods such as pot-roasted chicken with onions and potatoes, macaroni and cheese with broccoli, and mixed berry shortcake—dishes that grace the menus of fine New American dining destinations. You'll enjoy such creative twists on the classics as sautéed pork tenderloin with gingered apples, jasmine rice with shredded zucchini, and ginger biscuits. And you'll rediscover the delicious, old-fashioned goodness of retro and regional favorites such as crab cakes, spoon corn bread, and poached pears and blueberries.

Each recipe includes tips Chuck Williams has gleaned from experience over the years, along with suggestions that may spark your own ideas and varia-tions. At the back of the book there's also a special section that will help you develop your cooking techniques and methods.

Everything you need to begin cooking and eating simply and well is right here. It's that simple. Enjoy!

Chicken Soup with Celery and Lemon

1 small bunch celery
2 tablespoons unsalted butter
1 yellow onion, diced (1 cup/4 oz/125 g)
4 chicken thighs, 1¼–1½ lb (625–750 g) total weight
3 cups (24 fl oz/750 ml) chicken stock
3 cups (24 fl oz/750 ml) water
1 bay leaf
4 or 5 fresh thyme sprigs
2 or 3 fresh parsley sprigs
4 lemon zest strips, each 3–4 inches (7.5–10 cm) long by 1 inch (2.5 cm) wide
  (see page 122)
¼ teaspoon salt, or to taste
Freshly ground pepper
Juice of 1 lemon
Chopped fresh parsley

★ Remove the large outer stalks from the celery bunch and set aside for another use; use only 4 or 5 medium-sized inner stalks and the small ones in the center. Reserve some leaves for garnish. Separate the stalks and slice thinly, including the remaining leaves. You should have about 2 cups (8 oz/250 g). Set aside.

★ In a large saucepan over medium-low heat, melt the butter. Add the onion and sauté, stirring, until translucent, 3–4 minutes. Stir in the celery and set aside.

★ Rinse the chicken thighs and place in another saucepan. Add the chicken stock and the water. Bring to a boil and, using a skimmer or kitchen spoon, remove the scum from the surface. Transfer the chicken and its liquid to the pan holding the onions and celery.

★ To assemble a bouquet garni, gather together the bay leaf, thyme sprigs, parsley sprigs, and lemon zest strips and tie securely with kitchen string. Add to the pan along with the salt and pepper to taste and bring to a boil. Reduce the heat to low, cover, and simmer until the chicken and vegetables are tender, about 45 minutes.

★ Discard the bouquet garni. Using a kitchen spoon, skim off the fat from the surface. Stir in half of the lemon juice, taste and add more if needed, along with more salt and pepper if needed. Serve in warmed individual bowls with a whole thigh in each bowl. Garnish with parsley and celery leaves. Alternatively, transfer the thighs to a plate, remove the skin and bones, cut up the meat, and return it to the soup before serving.

NOTES

This chicken soup reminds me of the ones my grandmother made when I was a child, especially when I had to stay home from school with a cold. To add more citrus flavor to this soup, place a thin slice of lemon on top of each serving with a few sprigs of the parsley and celery leaves.

For a fresh-tasting, clear soup, it is important to remove all the scum that rises to the surface when you bring the chicken thighs to a boil, and then to skim off the fat when the soup is done. If you have the time to make the chicken stock from scratch, do so. Combine 1–2 pounds (500 g–1 kg) chicken parts (wings, backs, and necks); 1 carrot, 1 onion, and 1 celery stalk, all cut into chunks; a bay leaf; a pinch of dried thyme; salt; pepper; and water to cover. Simmer for about 1 hour, skimming regularly, and strain.

But if time is short, don't hesitate to use canned stock. Be aware, however, that some canned stocks are salty and you may not need to salt the soup further.

SERVES 4

White Bean Soup

2 cups (1 lb/500 g) dried Great Northern beans
1 smoked ham shank or ham hock, 3/4–1 lb (375–500 g)
1 small yellow onion stuck with 3 whole cloves
1 bay leaf
3 fresh oregano or thyme sprigs
3 large fresh parsley sprigs
1 celery stalk with leaves, cut into 2 or 3 pieces
1/2 lb (250 g) ripe plum (Roma) tomatoes
1 carrot, peeled and sliced (1/2 cup/2 oz/60 g)
1 sweet red (Spanish) onion or other sweet onion, diced
  (1 cup/4 oz/125 g)
1 teaspoon salt
Freshly ground pepper

★ Sort through the beans, discarding any impurities or discolored beans. Rinse the beans, drain, and put into a large pot. Add hot tap water to cover by 2–3 inches (5–7.5 cm). Bring just to a simmer and remove from the heat. Cover and let soak for 1–1½ hours. Drain, rinse, and drain again.

★ Return the beans to the pot and add 6 cups (48 fl oz/1.5 l) hot tap water. Rinse the ham shank or hock and add to the pot along with the yellow onion pierced with cloves. To assemble a bouquet garni, gather together the bay leaf, oregano or thyme sprigs, and parsley sprigs. Sandwich the bouquet between the 2 or 3 celery pieces and tie securely with kitchen string. Add to the pot. Bring just to a boil, reduce the heat to low, cover, and simmer for 45 minutes.

★ Meanwhile, core and peel the tomatoes (see page 123). Cut in half crosswise and carefully squeeze out the seeds. Cut into small chunks; you should have about 1 cup (6 oz/185 g). Set aside.

★ At the end of the 45-minute cooking time for the beans, remove the yellow onion and the bouquet garni and discard. Remove the ham shank or hock and, when cool enough to handle, cut the meat from the bone, removing and discarding any fat. Discard the bone and chop or shred the meat into small pieces. Return to the pot along with the tomatoes, carrot, and 1/2 cup (2 oz/60 g) of the sweet onion. Add the salt and freshly ground pepper to taste. Cover and simmer until the beans are completely tender, about 30 minutes longer.

★ Taste and adjust the seasonings. Serve in large individual bowls with the remaining sweet onion sprinkled evenly over the top.

(see page 123)

NOTES

Various versions of this soup have been part of American cooking since colonial times; in fact, the U.S. Senate dining room is famous for its white bean soup. Easy to make, this soup is a big help to those on a busy schedule. Feel free to substitute small white (navy) beans for the Great Northern beans.

I find that most dried beans can be treated in one of two ways: Soak them for 3–4 hours in cold water to cover before draining and cooking in fresh water. Or bring the beans and hot tap water to cover to a simmer, remove from the heat, cover, and let stand for 1–1½ hours before draining and continuing with the recipe.

SERVES 4–6

Roasted Red Pepper Soup

2–2¹/₂ lb (1–1.25 kg) red bell peppers (capsicums) (6 or 7)
3 tablespoons extra-virgin olive oil or vegetable oil
1 large yellow onion, chopped (1¹/₂ cups/6 oz/185 g)
1 cup (8 fl oz/250 ml) chicken stock
2 cups (16 fl oz/500 ml) water
1 teaspoon salt, or to taste
Pinch of red pepper flakes or cayenne pepper
1 tablespoon fresh lemon juice
8–10 fresh basil leaves, shredded
¹/₃–¹/₂ cup (3–4 fl oz/80–125 ml) heavy (double) cream

★ Roast and peel the bell peppers *(see page 121)*. Chop the peppers into medium pieces; set aside.

★ In a large saucepan over medium-low heat, warm the oil. Add the onion and sauté, stirring occasionally, until translucent, 3–4 minutes; do not allow to brown. Add the chicken stock, the water, salt, and red pepper flakes. Cover partially and bring to a boil. Reduce the heat to low and simmer until the onion is tender, about 15–20 minutes. Add the roasted peppers and cook for 10 minutes longer.

★ Place a colander over a large bowl. Drain the peppers and onion in the colander, reserving the liquid. Working in batches, transfer the peppers and onion to a food processor fitted with the metal blade or to a blender. Pulse a few times to achieve a textured purée.

★ Return the purée and the reserved liquid to the saucepan and reheat over medium heat. Cook, stirring, for 3–4 minutes. Stir in the lemon juice and cook for 1 minute longer. Taste and adjust the seasonings. Stir in about one-third of the shredded basil.

★ Ladle the soup into warmed individual bowls. Float 1–2 tablespoons cream on each serving and then sprinkle with the remaining basil. Serve immediately.

NOTES

Make this colorful soup during the summer, when red bell peppers are most abundant in the market. You can serve it cold as well as hot; it tastes even better after being refrigerated overnight. Turn any leftover soup into a rich cream soup by stirring in an equal quantity of milk or cream and seasoning to taste.

If you are rushed for time, you can skip the roasting and peeling of the peppers. Simply halve, stem, and seed them, cut them into medium pieces, and add them to the saucepan with the onions. In this case, don't purée the vegetables in a food processor or blender; instead, pass them, along with their cooking liquid, through a food mill fitted with a medium or fine disk *(see page 121)*.

SERVES 4

Zucchini Soup

NOTES

This simple summertime soup makes a pleasant start to a meal. It is rather thick, so add more milk or chicken stock if you prefer it thinner. You can also add a finely shredded carrot to the soup if you like, or add 8–12 small peeled and deveined shrimp (prawns) during the last 4–5 minutes of cooking.

It's worth the little extra time to salt and drain the shredded zucchini. The step removes a slight edge of bitterness. Most of the salt washes away in the squeezing and rinsing.

SERVES 4

1 1/2–2 lb (750 g–1 kg) small zucchini (courgettes)
Salt
2 tablespoons unsalted butter
2 yellow onions, diced (2 cups/8 oz/250 g)
2 cups (16 fl oz/500 ml) chicken stock
Freshly grated nutmeg
2 teaspoons finely chopped fresh mint
3 cups (24 fl oz/750 ml) milk
Freshly ground pepper
1/2 teaspoon fresh lemon juice, or to taste
4 thin lemon slices

★ Trim the zucchini and shred on a medium-holed shredder; you should have 6–7 cups. Alternatively, use the shredding disk of a food processor. In a colander set over a bowl, layer half of the zucchini. Sprinkle with salt, then top with the remaining zucchini and again sprinkle with salt. Set aside for 25–30 minutes to drain off the bitter liquid.

★ Pick up the drained zucchini by small handfuls and squeeze out the released juice. Return the zucchini to the colander and rinse under cold running water to wash out the salt. Again, squeeze out the moisture by handfuls, then set aside.

★ In a large saucepan over medium-low heat, melt the butter. Add the onion and sauté, stirring, until translucent, 3–4 minutes. Add the chicken stock, cover, and simmer until the onion is tender, 15–20 minutes. Transfer the onion and liquid to a food processor fitted with the metal blade or to a blender; purée until smooth.

★ Return the onion purée to the pan and add the zucchini, a pinch of nutmeg, and 1 teaspoon of the mint. Bring to a simmer, cover, and simmer for 6–8 minutes. Add the milk and season with salt, if needed, pepper, and the 1/2 teaspoon lemon juice or more to taste. Heat until very hot but do not allow to boil. Taste and adjust the seasonings again.

★ Ladle into warmed individual bowls. Sprinkle with the remaining mint and garnish each serving with a slice of lemon.

Tomato-Leek Soup with Dill

2 leeks
3 tablespoons extra-virgin olive oil or vegetable oil
2 cloves garlic, coarsely chopped
2 tablespoons water
2 lb (1 kg) ripe plum (Roma) tomatoes, cored and coarsely chopped
1 medium potato, preferably baking variety, peeled and coarsely chopped
1 tablespoon chopped fresh dill, plus chopped fresh dill for garnish
$1/2$ teaspoon salt
$1/8$ teaspoon red pepper flakes
$1/2$ lemon
$1/2$ cup (4 fl oz/125 ml) sour cream

★ Trim the leeks, leaving some of the tender green tops intact. Make a lengthwise slit along each leek to within about 2 inches (5 cm) of the root end. Place under running water to wash away any dirt lodged between the leaves. Cut crosswise into slices $1/2$ inch (12 mm) thick. You should have about 2 cups (8 oz/250 g). Set aside.

★ In a large saucepan over low heat, warm the oil. Add the garlic and sauté gently for 2 minutes. Add the leeks, raise the heat to medium, and sauté, stirring, until soft, 3–4 minutes. Add the water, stir, cover, and cook over medium-low heat for about 4–5 minutes longer. Do not allow to boil dry; add water as necessary.

★ Add the tomatoes, potato, the 1 tablespoon dill, salt, and red pepper flakes to the pan. Cook uncovered over medium heat, stirring constantly, until the juices start to release, about 2–3 minutes. Then cover and cook, stirring occasionally, until the tomatoes are soft and the leeks and potato are tender when pierced with a fork, about 15–20 minutes longer.

★ Remove from the heat. Pass the soup through a food mill (see page 121). Alternatively, force the soup through a coarse-mesh sieve. Return the puréed soup to the pan and place over medium heat. Bring to a simmer. Squeeze a little juice from the lemon half into the soup, taking care to keep seeds out. Taste and adjust the seasonings. If a thinner soup is desired, add water.

★ Ladle the soup into warmed individual bowls. Float 2 tablespoons sour cream on top of each serving. Garnish with chopped dill.

NOTES

If you grow tomatoes in your back-yard and end up with a bumper crop during the summer, or simply find fresh vine-ripened tomatoes at an unbeatable price at your local market, this is a recipe to remember.

If leeks are unavailable, use 2 cups (8 oz/250 g) coarsely chopped yellow onion.

This is one soup that truly benefits from using a food mill for puréeing. If you like to make soup, it is worth it to make the small investment in a food mill, which simplifies the preparation of many different puréed soups. In the case of this recipe, passing the soup through a food mill produces an even consistency while removing the tomatoes' skins and seeds and any tough leek fibers. If you don't have a food mill and want to use a food processor or blender instead, force the soup through a medium sieve after puréeing.

SERVES 4

Easy Vegetable Soup

NOTES

You can vary the ingredients in this versatile soup recipe according to whatever is in season. Choose the vegetables you like best. Just be sure they go well together. Green peas can replace the green beans, and turnips can replace the carrots. Feel free to add zucchini (courgettes), bell pepper (capsicum), chickpeas (garbanzo beans), or pasta.

To save time, cut up the vegetables ahead of time. Don't cook the soup too long after you've added all the vegetables: The freshness of their flavor is most important here.

SERVES 4

1 lb (500 g) ripe plum (Roma) tomatoes
2 tablespoons unsalted butter
1 yellow onion, diced (1 cup/4 oz/125 g)
2 cups (16 fl oz/500 ml) chicken stock
4 cups (32 fl oz/1 l) water
1 bay leaf
3 fresh oregano sprigs
2 fresh parsley sprigs
2 lemon zest strips, each 2 inches (5 cm) long by 1 inch (2.5 cm) wide *(see page 122)*
1/2 cup (2 oz/60 g) thinly sliced carrot
1 lb (500 g) red new potatoes, unpeeled, cut into 1-inch (2.5-cm) cubes
1/2 cup (2 1/2 oz/75 g) diced celery, including the leaves
1/2 teaspoon salt, or to taste
Freshly ground pepper
1 ear yellow corn, husk and silk removed, trimmed of any defects
1/4 lb (125 g) small green beans, trimmed and sliced 1 inch (2.5 cm) thick on the diagonal (1 cup)

★ Core and peel the tomatoes *(see page 123)*. Cut in half crosswise and carefully squeeze out the seeds. Cut into small pieces. Set aside.

★ In a large saucepan over medium-low heat, melt the butter. Add the onion and sauté, stirring, until translucent, 3–4 minutes. Add the chicken stock and water. To assemble a bouquet garni, gather together the bay leaf, oregano sprigs, parsley sprigs, and lemon zest strips and tie securely with kitchen string. Add to the pan along with the tomatoes, carrot, potatoes, celery, and the salt and pepper to taste. Bring just to a simmer over medium-high heat, then reduce the heat to low, cover, and simmer for 20 minutes.

★ Firmly hold the ear of corn, stem end down, on a cutting surface and, using a sharp knife, carefully cut off the kernels. Add the kernels to the soup along with the green beans and continue to simmer, covered, for another 15 minutes.

★ Remove and discard the bouquet garni. Taste and adjust the seasonings. Serve very hot.

Broiled Shrimp and Spinach Salad

1 lb (500 g) medium shrimp (prawns) in the shell (about 24)
2 $\frac{1}{8}$ teaspoons salt, or to taste
$\frac{1}{2}$ lb (250 g) young, small green beans, trimmed
$\frac{1}{2}$ lb (250 g) baby spinach leaves, or 1 bunch young, tender spinach
1 $\frac{1}{2}$ tablespoons fresh lemon juice
$\frac{1}{3}$ cup (3 fl oz/80 ml) extra-virgin olive oil
2 teaspoons minced fresh dill
Freshly ground pepper
1 tablespoon minced green (spring) onion, including some tender green tops

★ Preheat a broiler (griller).

★ Peel, devein, and butterfly the shrimp *(see page 123)*. Place the shrimp in a bowl and add water to cover. Add 1 teaspoon of the salt, stir to dissolve, and let stand for 10 minutes. Drain, rinse, and drain again; dry on paper towels. Set aside.

★ Bring a saucepan three-fourths full of water to a boil. Add the green beans and 1 teaspoon salt and bring back to a boil. Cook until tender but still crisp, 4–5 minutes. Drain and immediately plunge into cold water to stop the cooking. Drain again and set aside.

★ Rinse the baby spinach leaves and dry. If using bunch spinach, pick over the leaves, discarding tough and large ones, and remove the stems. Wash and dry well. If the leaves are large, tear them into small pieces. Place the spinach in a bowl.

★ To make the vinaigrette, in a small bowl, combine the lemon juice and the remaining $\frac{1}{8}$ teaspoon salt and stir to dissolve. Add the olive oil, dill, and pepper to taste and whisk until blended. Stir in the green onion and set aside.

★ Arrange the shrimp in a small broiling pan without a rack or in a flameproof baking dish. Brush the shrimp with a little of the vinaigrette and place under the broiler about 3 inches (7.5 cm) from the heat. Broil (grill) until the shrimp turn pink, turning once, 3–4 minutes. Remove from the broiler and add the remaining vinaigrette and the green beans to the pan or dish. Stir to coat the shrimp and beans with the vinaigrette. Using tongs, transfer the shrimp and beans to a plate.

★ Pour the vinaigrette over the spinach and toss quickly. Divide the spinach among individual plates and arrange the shrimp and green beans on top. Serve at once.

NOTES

Light salads combining hot seafood or chicken with fresh greens is one of California's best contributions to American cooking. Add a good soup and a simple fruit dessert and you have a perfect weekend lunch or weekday supper.

If unable to find baby spinach, pick out a bunch of spinach that has lots of small, tender leaves, and take care to wash them thoroughly.

Peel the shrimp and then soak them in salted water for 10–15 minutes to freshen them and eliminate any strong odor. After soaking, rinse well in fresh water before use.

SERVES 4

Tropical Salad with Lime Dressing

2 ripe avocados
1 large or 2 small, ripe papayas
1 English (hothouse) cucumber, or 1 or 2 regular cucumbers
1 head romaine lettuce
2 limes
1/8 teaspoon salt
Freshly ground pepper
1/2 cup (4 fl oz/125 ml) extra-virgin olive oil
2–3 teaspoons honey

★ Halve each avocado and remove the pit. Peel the halves and cut each lengthwise into 5 or 6 slices.

★ Halve the papaya(s) and remove the seeds. Peel the papaya halves and then cut lengthwise into thin slices.

★ Peel the cucumber, cut in half crosswise, and then slice in half lengthwise. Using a melon baller or small spoon, scoop out the seeds and discard. Cut crosswise into slices 1/2 inch (12 mm) thick.

★ Separate the lettuce leaves from the head and pick out 8 of the best ones; save the remaining leaves for another use. Wash and dry well.

★ Using a zester or fine-holed shredder, and holding each lime over a saucer, shred the zest (green part only) from the skin *(see page 122)*. Cut each lime in half and squeeze the juice from all 4 lime halves; you will need 2 tablespoons. Set aside.

★ On individual plates, make an attractive arrangement of the lettuce, avocado, papaya, and cucumber slices, dividing them evenly. Sprinkle the shredded lime zest over the top.

★ In a bowl, combine the 2 tablespoons lime juice, the salt, and pepper to taste. Stir well to dissolve the salt. Add the olive oil and 2 teaspoons honey and whisk until well blended. Taste and adjust the seasonings, adding more honey if desired.

★ Spoon the dressing over the salad or pass in a bowl at the table.

NOTES

California-grown avocados are the best choice for this refreshing salad. The Hass avocado, with bumpy green-black skin, is available in summer; Fuerte avocados, with smooth green skins, are available in winter. Simply holding an avocado in your hand will tell you if the flesh is turning soft beneath the skin, a sign of ripeness. Unless you plan to make the salad immediately, select avocados that are just beginning to ripen and feel only slightly soft. All avocados bruise easily, especially when close to being ripe; choose ones with no visible bruises.

English hothouse cucumbers are much milder in flavor than other cucumbers, they have thinner skins and very small seeds. In fact, you don't even have to peel them or remove the seeds if you want to skip that step.

When making the vinaigrette, dissolve the salt in the lime juice before adding the oil, as the oil prevents the salt from dissolving fully.

SERVES 4

Asparagus Mimosa Salad

SERVES 4

NOTES

Take care not to overcook the asparagus; the stalks should be tender-crisp. I think the best way to cook slender young asparagus stalks is in a sauté pan or frying pan large enough to hold them perfectly flat and fully covered in boiling water. For medium to large stalks, use a vertical asparagus pot. It holds the stalks upright, allowing the tender tips to steam while the tougher bottoms boil in water.

The chopped egg whites and sieved yolks that garnish the asparagus are said to resemble mimosa flowers, giving the salad its name. Some people have trouble keeping the hard-cooked yolks from taking on a greenish color. The secret to keeping them bright yellow is to start with very fresh eggs and, once they are boiled, transfer them immediately to a bowl of cold water.

For the dressing, choose an extra-virgin olive oil with a mild flavor so that it won't mask the delicacy of the tarragon-flavored white wine vinegar.

1 red bell pepper (capsicum)
2 eggs, at room temperature
1½ lb (750 g) asparagus
Salt
2 tablespoons white tarragon vinegar
½ cup (4 fl oz/125 ml) mild extra-virgin olive oil
2 tablespoons minced green (spring) onion, including some tender green tops
Freshly ground pepper
¼ cup (2 oz/60 g) well-drained capers

★ Roast and peel the bell pepper (*see page 121*). Cut the pepper into long, narrow strips and set aside.

★ To hard-cook the eggs, make a tiny hole in one end of the shell with a pin or needle to help avoid cracking. Place the eggs in a saucepan and add water to cover. Place over medium heat and bring to a boil; reduce the heat to low and simmer for 15 minutes. Immediately plunge the eggs into cold water. When cool enough to handle, crack each shell and then roll each egg around in the palm of your hand to crack it evenly all over. Peel off the shell. Separate the whites from the yolks. Coarsely chop the whites; cover and set aside. Using the back of a wooden spoon, force the yolks through a coarse-mesh sieve into a bowl; cover and set aside.

★ Cut or break off the tough white ends of the asparagus. Trim all to the same length. If the asparagus are large, peel the tough skin from the stalk as well: Using a vegetable peeler and starting 2 inches (5 cm) below the tip, peel off the thin outer skin. Bring a large sauté pan or frying pan half full of water to a boil. Add 1 teaspoon salt and the asparagus, return to a boil, reduce the heat slightly, and simmer, uncovered, until tender but still crisp, 6–9 minutes, depending upon their size. Drain and immediately plunge into cold water to stop the cooking. Drain again, pat dry with paper towels, and set aside.

★ In a small bowl, stir together the vinegar and ⅛ teaspoon salt until the salt dissolves. Add the olive oil and whisk until well blended. Stir in the green onion and pepper to taste.

★ Arrange the asparagus on a serving plate or individual plates. Carefully spoon the dressing over the asparagus, particularly over the tips and the upper part of the spears. Spoon the chopped egg whites over the asparagus, in a crosswise band, and then spoon the yolks on top of the whites. Arrange the red pepper strips over the asparagus and garnish the egg yolks with the capers.

Chicken Salad with Apple and Walnuts

1/2 cup (2 oz/60 g) coarsely chopped walnuts

1 large or 2 small bunches watercress

1 large tart apple such as Granny Smith

1/2 lemon, plus 1 tablespoon fresh lemon juice

Salt and freshly ground pepper

1/4 cup (2 fl oz/60 ml) good-quality toasted walnut oil

4 chicken breast halves, 8–9 oz (250–280 g) each, skinned and boned
(5–6 oz/155–185 g when boned) *(see page 124)*

2 tablespoons unsalted butter

2 tablespoons extra-virgin olive oil

2 or 3 celery stalks with leaves, preferably the tender center stalks,
thinly sliced crosswise (1/2–3/4 cup/2–3 oz/60–90 g)

★ Preheat an oven to 325°F (165°C). Spread the walnuts on a baking sheet and bake until they begin to change color, 6–8 minutes. Watch carefully so they do not burn. Set aside to cool.

★ Wash the watercress carefully. Discard the main stems and any yellow or old leaves. You should have about 6 cups (6 oz/185 g). Dry well, place in a salad bowl, cover with a damp kitchen towel, and refrigerate for 20–30 minutes.

★ Peel, quarter, and core the apple. Cut the quarters in half crosswise and then thinly slice lengthwise. Place in a bowl. Squeeze the juice from the 1/2 lemon over the top to keep them from turning brown. Toss to coat well. Set aside.

★ In a small bowl, stir together the 1 tablespoon lemon juice, 1/8 teaspoon salt, and pepper to taste until the salt dissolves completely. Whisk in the walnut oil until well blended. Set aside.

★ Remove all fat from the chicken breasts. Rinse the breasts and dry with paper towels. Place each breast between 2 sheets of plastic wrap and, using a rolling pin, flatten to an even thickness. Season with salt and pepper. In a large sauté pan (preferably nonstick) over medium-high heat, melt the butter with the olive oil. When hot, add the chicken breasts and sauté, turning once, until lightly browned and opaque throughout when pierced with a sharp knife, 3 1/2–4 minutes on each side. Transfer to a plate and keep warm.

★ Add the celery, apple, and half of the walnuts to the watercress. Whisk the dressing again, pour over the salad, and toss well. Divide among 4 individual plates. Slice the warm chicken breasts crosswise into strips 1/2 inch (12 mm) wide and arrange over the salads. Sprinkle with the remaining walnuts and serve.

Taking the basic ingredients of the famous Waldorf salad—apples, celery, and walnuts—and combining them with strips of freshly sautéed chicken breast brings a new twist to this classic salad. By substituting a light vinaigrette made with fresh lemon juice—which keeps the apples from discoloring—for the Waldorf's traditional mayonnaise-based dressing, you can create the kind of fresh-tasting, light lunch that many people crave.

If you have never tried walnut oil, this is a great opportunity to taste it. Seek out a good oil pressed from lightly toasted nuts, light in color and flavor. Some walnut oils are dark and strong tasting, and if that is all you can find, I suggest using extra-virgin olive oil instead. Once opened, the walnut oil should be refrigerated.

Take care not to overtoast the walnuts that garnish the salad; they're ready just when they start to change color.

SERVES 4

Garden Greens and Citrus Salad

¹/₂ cup (2 oz/60 g) coarsely chopped pecans or walnuts

1 orange

1 pink grapefruit

8–10 oz (250–315 g) small garden lettuces, or a combination of romaine, butter, and
    chicory lettuces

1 tablespoon peach vinegar or other fruit-flavored vinegar

¹/₈ teaspoon salt

Freshly ground pepper

¹/₃ cup (3 fl oz/80 ml) extra-virgin olive oil

2 teaspoons honey

¹/₂ cup (3 oz/90 g) crumbled feta cheese, preferably made from sheep's milk

2 or 3 thin slices sweet red (Spanish) onion or other sweet onion, separated into rings

★ Preheat an oven to 325°F (165°C). Spread out the nuts on a baking sheet and bake until they begin to change color, 6–8 minutes. Watch carefully so they do not burn. Remove from the oven and set aside to cool.

★ Peel and section the orange and grapefruit (see page 122). Set aside.

★ If using small garden lettuces, pick over and discard any old leaves. Wash and dry well (if lettuces are not purchased already washed). If using other lettuces, discard tough outer leaves, wash and dry thoroughly, and tear into bite-sized pieces. Place in a large bowl.

★ In a small bowl, stir together the vinegar, salt, and pepper to taste until the salt dissolves. Add the olive oil and honey and whisk until well blended. Taste and adjust the seasonings. Drizzle the dressing over the lettuce and toss to coat well.

★ Divide the lettuce among individual plates. Arrange the orange and grapefruit segments among the leaves. Sprinkle on the feta cheese and nuts, scatter on the onion rings, and serve.

NOTES

Tender, crisp little salad leaves give this recipe a pleasing variety of tastes, colors, and shapes.

Seek out a fruit-flavored vinegar for the dressing. I do not mean vinegars made from fruit, most notably pear vinegar, which are regional specialties of the northeastern and northwestern United States. Rather, I am talking about infusions of raspberries, peaches, or other fruits in mild wine vinegars—delicious additions to salad dressings and to sauces for chicken, pork, and veal. Such vinegars are becoming increasingly available in food stores and specialty shops.

SERVES 4

Corn and Red Pepper Salad

1 large red bell pepper (capsicum)

1 1/8 teaspoons salt

4 ears yellow corn, husks and silks removed, trimmed of any defects

2 tablespoons minced green (spring) onion, including some tender green tops

1 tablespoon white tarragon vinegar

3 tablespoons extra-virgin olive oil

Freshly ground pepper

Romaine or butter lettuce

★ Roast and peel the bell pepper *(see page 121)*. Cut the pepper lengthwise into strips 1/4 inch (6 mm) wide and then cut the strips in half crosswise. You should have about 1 cup (5 oz/155 g). Set aside.

★ Bring a large pot three-fourths full of water to a boil. Add 1 teaspoon of the salt and the corn to the boiling water, cover partially, and boil for 5 minutes. Remove the corn and immediately plunge into cold water to stop the cooking. When cool enough to handle, firmly hold each ear of corn, stem end down, on a cutting surface. Using a sharp knife, carefully cut off the kernels. You should have 3 cups (18 oz/560 g).

★ Place the corn kernels, pepper strips, and green onion in a bowl and stir together. In a small bowl, stir together the vinegar and the remaining 1/8 teaspoon salt until the salt dissolves. Add the olive oil and freshly ground pepper to taste and whisk until well blended. Pour the dressing over the corn mixture and stir until well blended. Taste and adjust the seasonings. At this point the corn mixture can be covered and refrigerated for 1 or 2 hours.

★ To serve, arrange lettuce leaves on a serving plate or 4 individual plates and place the corn mixture in the center.

NOTES

Bright in both color and flavor, this salad serves as a good accompaniment to cold meats or grilled chicken or fish. When tomatoes are ripe and plentiful, try serving it inside the tomatoes: Slice off the tops of the tomatoes, scoop out their seeds and membranes, and spoon in the salad.

If you have never tasted tarragon-flavored wine vinegar, I suggest you sample this delicately perfumed seasoning; it's available in most specialty-food stores. The best version is made with Champagne vinegar; however, those made with white wine vinegar are preferable to those made with red wine vinegar.

I think it is best to cook the ears of corn before cutting off their kernels. The kernels cook better and stay moister.

SERVES 4

Caesar Salad

1 or 2 heads romaine lettuce, depending upon size, preferably with small leaves

3 or 4 slices French or Italian bread, each $^3/_8$ inch (9 mm) thick

3 tablespoons extra-virgin olive oil, plus $^1/_2$ cup (4 fl oz/125 ml)

2 cloves garlic

Salt

6–8 good-quality anchovy fillets in olive oil, drained

1$^1/_2$ teaspoons dry mustard

2 tablespoons fresh lemon juice

1$^1/_2$ tablespoons plain yogurt

$^1/_2$ cup (2 oz/60 g) freshly grated Parmesan cheese

Freshly ground pepper

★ Break off the leaves from the lettuce stalk, discarding the bruised ones and reserving large outer leaves for another use. Separate the smaller inner leaves and wash and dry well. Break into halves or thirds. Place in a salad bowl, cover with a damp kitchen towel, and refrigerate for 20–30 minutes to crisp.

★ Remove the crusts from the bread slices and discard. Cut the bread into $^1/_2$-inch (12-mm) cubes. You should have approximately 2 cups (4 oz/125 g).

★ In a large frying pan over low heat, warm the 3 tablespoons olive oil. Using the flat side of a chopping knife, smash 1 of the garlic cloves and add to the oil. Sauté for 1–2 minutes. Add the bread cubes and fry, stirring and tossing, until crisp and golden on all sides, 4–5 minutes. Discard the garlic. Sprinkle the bread cubes with a little salt. Using a slotted spoon, transfer to paper towels to drain. Set aside to cool.

★ Chop the remaining garlic clove and combine with the $^1/_2$ cup (4 fl oz/125 ml) olive oil in a blender. Purée until smooth. In a small bowl, and using a fork, mash the anchovies until they form a paste. Add to the oil and garlic in the blender along with the mustard, lemon juice, and yogurt. Blend at high speed until a smooth emulsion forms. Add 2 tablespoons of the Parmesan cheese and blend again. Season with a little salt, remembering that anchovies are salty, and a little pepper.

★ Add three-fourths of the dressing to the lettuce and toss to coat well. Add about half of the remaining cheese and toss again. Taste and add more dressing or more seasonings to taste. Sprinkle with the toasted croutons and the remaining cheese. Serve immediately.

NOTES

So many versions of Caesar salad exist today that it's hard to tell what is authentic. I still like the flavor of the one reputed to be the original, as created by the Tijuana chef César Cárdenas: a salad of crisp romaine lettuce and garlic croutons coated with a tart dressing of lemon juice, garlic, Parmesan cheese, and anchovy bound in a light emulsion with coddled (lightly boiled) egg.

With this version, I have left the egg out and have instead used plain yogurt to create the creamy emulsion. One thing I wouldn't dream of changing, though, is the anchovy; many versions omit it, but I like a good anchovy flavor in my Caesar salad, as well as the taste of imported Parmesan. Be sure to seek out high-quality anchovies, as some brands can be overly strong in flavor.

It's also important to make fresh croutons. There's nothing worse in a salad than stale bread cubes. Sautéing the croutons in good olive oil with garlic is quick and easy.

SERVES 4

Baked Chicken with Honey-Lemon Glaze

1 lb (500 g) white boiling onions (about 24), 1 inch (2.5 cm) in diameter
1 lemon
1/4 cup (3 oz/90 g) light honey
3 teaspoons chopped fresh thyme
1 chicken, 3 1/2–4 lb (1.75–2 kg), preferably free-range, cut into serving pieces
3 tablespoons unsalted butter
2 tablespoons minced shallot
Salt and freshly ground pepper
1/2 cup (3 oz/90 g) golden raisins (sultanas)

★ Position a rack in the middle of an oven and preheat to 375°F (190°C).

★ Trim and cut a cross in the root end of each onion. Peel the onions and put into a saucepan. Add water to cover and bring to a boil. Reduce the heat to medium-low and simmer, uncovered, for 5 minutes. Drain and set aside.

★ Using a zester or fine-holed shredder, shred the zest from the lemon (see page 122). Then squeeze the juice into another bowl. Measure 2 tablespoons of the juice and add to the zest. Stir in the honey and 2 teaspoons of the thyme. Set aside.

★ Remove any excess fat from the chicken pieces. Cut each breast in half crosswise. Be sure the drumsticks and thighs are separated. Remove wing tips and discard. Rinse the chicken pieces and pat dry with paper towels.

★ In a 2 1/2- to 3-qt (2.5- to 3-l) baking pan that holds the chicken comfortably in one layer. Combine the butter and shallot in the pan; place in the oven for 1–2 minutes to melt the butter. Add the chicken pieces and turn to coat well; leave the pieces skin-side down. Sprinkle with salt and pepper and the remaining 1 teaspoon thyme. Bake uncovered, basting a couple of times with the pan juices, for 15 minutes.

★ Turn the chicken skin-side up and add the onions and raisins to the pan. Baste the chicken and onions with half of the honey-lemon mixture. Return to the oven for 10 minutes. Baste with the remaining honey-lemon mixture, reduce the heat to 350°F (180°C), and continue to bake, basting every 7–8 minutes with the pan juices, until the chicken and onions are fork-tender and golden and the pan juices have thickened to a glaze, another 25–30 minutes. If the juices have not thickened, transfer the chicken pieces to a plate and boil the juices on the stove top until reduced to a glaze, 2–3 minutes. Return the chicken to the pan and turn several times in the glaze.

★ Arrange the chicken and onions on a serving platter. Spoon on the glaze and serve immediately.

NOTES

Seek out a fresh free-range chicken. (The term, by the way, doesn't mean that the chickens are free to roam; they're just raised in open areas and fed well.) A good poultry market will cut up the chicken just the way you want it. Have them trim off the excess fat from the breasts and thighs, and cut the breasts into halves. Reserve the back, neck, and giblets for another use or discard.

For good, juicy results, take care not to overbake the chicken. Start testing for doneness toward the end of the cooking time by piercing a breast at its thickest part with a sharp knife: The flesh should look opaque and the juices should run clear.

I find the lighter-colored honeys taste milder than the dark, and are preferable in this recipe. Fresh thyme will contribute the best flavor, too; but if you can't find it, feel free to substitute 1–1 1/2 teaspoons of the dried herb.

SERVES 4

Sautéed Chicken Breasts with Ginger-Orange Glaze

4 chicken breast halves, 8–9 oz (250–280 g) each, skinned and boned
  (5–6 oz/155–185 g when boned) *(see page 124)*
1/2 cup (2 1/2 oz/75 g) all-purpose (plain) flour
Salt and freshly ground pepper
2 tablespoons unsalted butter
1 tablespoon extra-virgin olive oil
1 tablespoon minced green (spring) onion, including some tender green tops
1 cup (8 fl oz/250 ml) fresh orange juice
1 tablespoon light brown sugar
1/2 teaspoon peeled and grated fresh ginger, or more for stronger flavor
2 teaspoons Dijon mustard
1 orange

★ Remove all excess fat from the chicken breasts. Rinse and pat dry with paper towels. Place each breast between 2 sheets of plastic wrap and, using a rolling pin, flatten to an even thickness. Put the flour on a plate or on a piece of waxed paper. Lightly sprinkle salt and pepper on each breast and then lightly coat with flour, shaking off any excess.

★ In a large sauté pan or frying pan (preferably nonstick) over medium heat, melt the butter with the olive oil. When hot, add the chicken and sauté, turning once, until lightly browned and opaque throughout when pierced with a knife, about 5 minutes on each side. Transfer to a plate and keep warm.

★ Pour off any excess fat from the pan and place the pan over medium-high heat. Add the green onion, orange juice, brown sugar, ginger, and Dijon mustard and mix well, scraping up any browned bits from the bottom. Cook, stirring, until thickened and reduced, about 5 minutes. Taste and adjust the seasonings.

★ Return the chicken to the pan and turn the breasts over several times to coat them well with the sauce. Transfer to a warmed serving plate or individual plates and spoon the remaining sauce over the breasts.

★ Using a zester or fine-holed shredder, and holding the orange directly over the chicken, shred the zest (orange part only) from the skin directly onto each breast *(see page 122)*. Serve immediately.

Roast Chicken with Apple and Sage

1 roasting chicken, 4–4½ lb (2–2.5 kg), preferably free-range
1 lemon, cut in half
Salt
½ yellow onion, cut into pieces
1 celery stalk with leaves, cut into pieces
1 small apple, cut into quarters
4 fresh sage sprigs
Crushed whole peppercorns or freshly ground pepper
2–3 tablespoons extra-virgin olive oil
1 cup (8 fl oz/250 ml) water

★ Position a rack in the lower part of an oven and preheat the oven to 425°F (220°C). Grease a rack in an open roasting pan, preferably a nonstick roasting pan with a V-shaped rack.

★ Remove giblets, if any, from the chicken cavity and put aside for another purpose. Remove all the excess fat from around the cavity opening and rinse the chicken inside and out. Dry thoroughly with paper towels. Rub the inside of the cavity with one of the lemon halves, squeezing out some of the juice as you do. Sprinkle the cavity lightly with salt and slip in the onion, celery, apple, 2 of the sage sprigs, both lemon halves, and a few crushed peppercorns or ground pepper. Close the cavity and secure with a short metal skewer or a sturdy toothpick. To truss the chicken, use kitchen string to tie the legs together and then tie the legs and wings close to the body. Brush the outside of the chicken with some of the oil and sprinkle with salt and pepper.

★ Place the chicken in the rack, breast side down. Add the water to the pan. Place in the oven and roast for 25 minutes. Turn the chicken breast-side up and brush with more oil. Tear the remaining 2 sage sprigs into small pieces and scatter over the breast. Reduce the heat to 400°F (200°C) and continue to roast, basting with the pan juices every 7–8 minutes, until golden brown, 30–40 minutes longer. To test for doneness, insert an instant-read thermometer in the thickest part of the breast or the thigh away from the bone; it should read 165°F (74°C) in the breast or 180°F (82°C) in the thigh.

★ Transfer to a warmed serving platter, cover loosely with aluminum foil, and let rest for 5–10 minutes before carving. Meanwhile, place the roasting pan on the stove top and, using a spoon, skim off the fat from the pan juices. Reheat the juices over medium heat, adding a little more water to the pan if only 1–2 tablespoons pan juices remain; scrape any browned bits from the pan bottom. Season to taste. Pass the pan juices in a bowl at the table.

NOTES

Start roasting the chicken with the breast side down for the first 25 minutes. This enables the thighs and back to cook faster while slowing down the cooking of the breast, so that the chicken cooks more evenly; it also keeps the breast moister. Olive oil brushed over the chicken before roasting adds a nice flavor and promotes a golden color.

SERVES 4–6

Poached Chicken Breasts with Tarragon

2 cups (16 fl oz/500 ml) chicken stock, or as needed

2 cups (16 fl oz/500 ml) dry white wine or water, or as needed

6 or 7 fresh tarragon sprigs, plus fresh tarragon leaves for garnish

1/2 yellow onion, cut in half

1 celery stalk, cut crosswise into quarters

1 teaspoon salt

4 or 5 peppercorns

2 or 3 lemon slices

4 chicken breast halves, 8–9 oz (250–280 g) each, skinned and boned (5–6 oz/155–185 g when boned) *(see page 124)*

2 tablespoons unsalted butter

2 tablespoons all-purpose (plain) flour

1/2 cup (4 fl oz/125 ml) heavy (double) cream

★ In a large sauté pan or wide saucepan that will accommodate the 4 chicken breasts without crowding, combine the chicken stock and wine or water. Add the tarragon sprigs, onion, celery, salt, peppercorns, and lemon slices. Bring to a boil, reduce the heat to low, cover, and simmer gently for 15–20 minutes to extract the flavor from the vegetables.

★ Remove all excess fat from the chicken breasts. Rinse the breasts, then place them in the pan, adding more stock or water if the breasts are not completely covered. Bring back just to a bare simmer (do not allow it to boil), cover (or cover partially), and poach gently until the breasts are tender and the flesh is opaque throughout when pierced with a sharp knife, 20–25 minutes. Alternatively, test the chicken with an instant-read thermometer; it should register 165°F (74°C) at its center. Transfer the breasts to a plate and keep warm. Strain the poaching liquid and reserve.

★ In a heavy saucepan (preferably nonstick) over medium-low heat, warm the butter until bubbling. Stir in the flour and cook, stirring, for a few seconds. While continuously stirring to avoid lumps, quickly add 1 cup (8 fl oz/250 ml) of the poaching liquid. Cook, stirring, until the mixture thickens and comes to a boil. Reduce the heat to low and cook for 1 minute longer, stirring a couple of times. Add the cream and stir until well blended. You should have a very smooth white sauce. Do not allow it to burn or stick.

★ Arrange the chicken breasts on individual plates and spoon the sauce evenly over the top to cover completely. Garnish with tarragon leaves.

NOTES

Subtly flavored, tender, low in fat, and easily prepared, poached chicken should be a regular item on everyone's home menu. If you want to make this particular recipe even lighter, substitute milk for the cream.

Although fresh tarragon imparts the best flavor to the poaching liquid, dried tarragon can be used if fresh is unavailable. Be sure the dried herb has a good green color and has not been sitting on your shelf for a long time. Use 2–3 teaspoons, and crush it in the palm of your hand with your thumb to develop its flavor before adding to the liquid.

SERVES 4

Fresh Chicken Sausages with Sweet Onions and Grapes

NOTES

Substitue turkey sausage for chicken, if you like. Turkey sausages are generally low in fat and full of flavor, not to mention quick and easy to prepare.

In this recipe, the tartness and lightness of the grapes complements the sausages and adds a touch of elegance that makes the dish suitable for serving at a small dinner party. Do not cook the grapes too long or they will begin to break down; they should just color slightly.

Accompany this dish with Spoon Corn Bread *(recipe on page 99)*, a tossed green salad, and fruit for dessert.

SERVES 4

2 tablespoons extra-virgin olive oil or vegetable oil

8 fresh chicken sausages such as chicken with apple, herbs, curry, or lemon, about 2 lb (1 kg)

¼ cup (2 fl oz/60 ml) dry white wine or apple juice

1 sweet red (Spanish) onion or other sweet onion, cut into chunks

2 cups (12 oz/375 g) ripe seedless white grapes

★ In a large sauté pan or frying pan over medium-high heat, warm the oil. When hot, add the sausages in a single layer, being careful not to crowd them. Cover partially (to help control splatter) and fry until nicely browned, 6–8 minutes on each side. Transfer to a warmed serving plate and keep warm.

★ Drain off the fat from the pan and add the wine or apple juice. Heat to bubbling over medium-high heat. Add the onion and sauté, stirring, for 1–2 minutes. Add the grapes and sauté, stirring often or shaking the pan to keep the grapes moving so they cook evenly, until they have colored a little, the onions have softened, and the liquid has evaporated, another 5–7 minutes.

★ Spoon the onion chunks and grapes over the sausages. Serve at once.

Curried Chicken Breasts with Basmati Rice

4 chicken breast halves, 8–9 oz (250–280 g) each, skinned and boned
(5–6 oz/155–185 g when boned) *(see page 124)*

2 tablespoons plus 1 teaspoon fresh lime juice, or as needed

1³/₄ cups (14 fl oz/440 ml) water

¹/₂ teaspoon salt, plus salt to taste

1 cup (7 oz/220 g) basmati rice, rinsed and drained

2 tablespoons unsalted butter

2 tablespoons extra-virgin olive oil

Freshly ground pepper

1 yellow onion, diced (1 cup/4 oz/125 g)

2–3 tablespoons curry powder, to taste

¹/₂ cup (4 fl oz/125 ml) chicken stock

1 cup (8 fl oz/250 ml) coconut milk or heavy (double) cream

1 tablespoon chopped fresh parsley

★ Remove any excess fat from the chicken breasts. Rinse and pat dry with paper towels. Slice crosswise into strips 1 inch (2.5 cm) wide. Place in a bowl, add the 2 tablespoons lime juice, and toss to coat. Set aside for about 15 minutes.

★ In a medium saucepan, combine the water and the ¹/₂ teaspoon salt. Bring to a boil and gradually add the rice. Reduce the heat to low, cover, and barely simmer until tender and the water is absorbed, 15–20 minutes. Remove from the heat and let stand, covered, for 5 minutes. Uncover, fluff with a fork, and re-cover until ready to serve.

★ Dry the chicken pieces with paper towels. In a large sauté pan or frying pan over medium-high heat, warm 1 tablespoon each of the butter and olive oil. When hot, add half of the chicken, sprinkle with salt and pepper, and sauté until golden, 2–3 minutes on each side. Transfer to a warm plate. Add the remaining 1 tablespoon each butter and oil to the pan and cook the remaining chicken. Transfer to the plate.

★ Pour off most of the fat and place the pan over low heat. Add the onion and sauté for 1 minute. Stir in the curry powder and sauté for 2 minutes longer. Stir in the chicken stock, scraping up any browned bits stuck to the bottom; cover and simmer over low heat for 5–6 minutes. Stir in the coconut milk or cream and continue to cook, uncovered, stirring occasionally, until slightly thickened, 1–2 minutes. Stir in the remaining 1 teaspoon lime juice and salt and pepper to taste. Return the chicken to the pan, stir to coat well, and heat through. Adjust the seasonings with more lime juice or salt and pepper.

★ Toss the rice with the parsley. Arrange the rice in a ring around the edge of a warmed platter. Spoon the chicken and sauce into the center and serve.

NOTES

A number of other small details will make a big difference in the quality of your curry. Start with a good, fresh curry powder, purchased in a small container from a food store that has a regular turnover in its stock; curry powder's flavor dissipates quickly, so it won't keep long on your shelf. Also, use basmati rice, available in most well-stocked food stores and ethnic markets; it has a delicately perfumed flavor and fluffy texture. If you can't find basmati, substitute a medium-grain white rice.

Finally, I find that curry gains a wonderful richness from coconut milk. This is not the watery liquid found inside coconuts, but rather a commercial product made by combining chopped coconut flesh with hot water and then straining the resulting thick, milky liquid through cheesecloth. You can find canned coconut milk in specialty-food shops and Asian markets

SERVES 4

Pot-Roasted Chicken with Onions and Potatoes

1 roasting chicken, $3^1/_2$–4 lb (1.75–2 kg), preferably free-range
2 lemons, cut into quarters
1 celery stalk, cut into pieces
4 or 5 fresh oregano sprigs
Salt and freshly ground pepper
2 lb (1 kg) small white boiling onions (about 48), 1 inch (2.5 cm) in diameter
2 lb (1 kg) small red new potatoes, unpeeled, halved, or quartered
4 tablespoons (2 oz/60 g) unsalted butter, at room temperature

★ Position a rack in the lower part of an oven and preheat to 425°F (220°C).

★ Remove the giblets, if any, from the chicken cavity and put aside for another purpose. Remove all excess fat from around the cavity opening and rinse the chicken inside and out. Dry thoroughly with paper towels. Slip 2 lemon quarters, the celery, and 2 or 3 oregano sprigs into the cavity. Sprinkle with a little salt and pepper. Close the opening with a small skewer or a sturdy wooden toothpick. To truss the chicken, use kitchen string to tie the legs together and then tie the legs and wings close to the body. Place in an ovenproof casserole or Dutch oven large and deep enough to accommodate it comfortably.

★ Trim and cut a cross in the root end of each onion, then peel the onions. Arrange the onions and potatoes around the chicken. Add 2 more lemon quarters and the remaining 2 or 3 oregano sprigs to the pot. Generously brush the chicken, onions, and potatoes with 2 tablespoons of the butter. Sprinkle to taste with salt and pepper.

★ Cover, place in the oven, and roast for 20 minutes. Reduce the heat to 325°F (165°C) and continue to roast, brushing with the remaining 2 tablespoons butter and then basting every 10 minutes with the pot juices, until the chicken is tender, about 1 hour longer. To check for doneness, insert an instant-read thermometer in the thickest part of the breast or thigh away from the bone; it should read 165°F (74°C) in the breast or 180°F (82°C) in the thigh.

★ Transfer the chicken to a warmed serving platter, cover loosely with aluminum foil, and let rest for 5–10 minutes before carving. Remove the oregano sprigs and lemon quarters from the pot and discard. Using a slotted spoon, remove the onions and potatoes from the pot and arrange around the perimeter of the platter. Garnish with the remaining 4 lemon quarters. Skim off the fat from the pot juices and discard. Reheat the juices to serving temperature and taste and adjust the seasonings. Pass the juices in a bowl at the table.

NOTES

Pot roasting dates back to the early days when ovens took constant watching and refueling; roasting in a covered heavy pot on top of the stove was much easier and more economical and reliable. Still a practical method today, pot roasting yields delicious results—either on top of the stove or in the oven. Its popularity can be measured by the steady interest in clay-pot cooking— essentially pot roasting in the oven.

Beef may come to mind first when pot roasting is mentioned, but chicken makes an equally good candidate. The poultry gains excellent flavor from the surrounding herbs and vegetables—an exchange of flavors and aromas that doesn't take place in an uncovered roasting pan. If you like, add other favorite vegetables such as sliced red bell pepper (capsicum), green beans, or tomatoes to the pot.

SERVES 4

Braised Brisket of Beef
with Port Wine

1 center-cut beef brisket, 3^1/$_2$–4 lb (1.75–2 kg)

3 tablespoons extra-virgin olive oil or vegetable oil

2 cloves garlic, chopped

1 yellow onion, chopped (1 cup/4 oz/125 g)

^{3}/$_4$ cup (4 oz/125 g) chopped celery

1 lb (500 g) ripe plum (Roma) tomatoes, cored and chopped (3 cups/14 oz/440 g)

3 whole cloves

2 orange zest strips, each 3 inches (7.5 cm) long by 1 inch (2.5 cm) wide *(see page 122)*

1 bay leaf

4 fresh thyme sprigs

3 fresh parsley sprigs

^{1}/$_2$ teaspoon salt, or to taste

Freshly ground pepper

1 cup (8 fl oz/250 ml) port wine

★ Position a rack in the lower part of an oven and preheat to 350°F (180°C).

★ Trim any excess fat from the beef. Select a large ovenproof pot or Dutch oven that will hold the meat comfortably. Add the oil and warm over medium-high heat. When hot, add the beef and brown on all sides, 4–5 minutes. Transfer to a plate and set aside. Reduce the heat to low, add the garlic and onion, and sauté until translucent, 3–4 minutes. Stir in the celery and tomatoes.

★ To make a bouquet garni, stick the cloves into the orange zest strips, then tie together the strips, bay leaf, thyme, and parsley with kitchen string. Add to the pot along with the salt, pepper to taste, the browned beef, and 1/2 cup (4 fl oz/125 ml) of the port. Cover tightly and place in the oven. Braise, basting frequently with the pan juices, until tender, 2–2^1/$_2$ hours. Transfer the meat to a warmed platter, cover loosely with aluminum foil, and keep warm.

★ Discard the bouquet garni. Rest a sieve over a bowl and pour in the pot contents, capturing the juices in the bowl. Transfer the vegetables in the sieve to a food processor fitted with the metal blade or to a blender. Purée until smooth.

★ Using a spoon, skim off the fat from the reserved juices. Return the juices and puréed vegetables to the pot, add the remaining ^{1}/$_2$ cup (4 fl oz/125 ml) port, and bring to a boil. Boil for a few seconds to dispel the alcohol. Adjust the seasonings.

★ Slice the meat about ^{1}/$_4$ inch (6 mm) thick. Spoon the sauce over the slices.

A classic of American cooking, braised brisket of beef was brought to this country by Jewish and other Eastern European immigrants. Many people today think they don't have the time to prepare this dish, but I like to think that the slow, moist braising method can actually save you time: With a little advance planning, you can set aside a bit of time to prepare this dish on the weekend using a larger cut of meat (4^1/$_2$–5 lb/ 2.25–2.5 kg), yielding enough leftovers for one or two easy meals later in the week. The braised meat reheats successfully, can also be made into a hash or combined with a sauce for pasta, or is delicious cold.

The best choice for braising is the center cut of brisket, but other tough, lean cuts such as chuck or rump roast are also excellent cooked this way. Seek out a local butcher to help you make the right choice. Serve the brisket with mashed potatoes, noodles, or rice to soak up the sauce.

SERVES 4–6
WITH LEFTOVERS

Veal Paprika

1 lb (500 g) ripe plum (Roma) tomatoes
2 lb (1 kg) boneless veal shoulder, cut into 1-inch (2.5-cm) cubes
2 tablespoons extra-virgin olive oil or vegetable oil, or as needed
1 yellow onion, diced (1 cup/4 oz/125 g)
1 green bell pepper (capsicum), seeded, deribbed, and diced (1 cup/5 oz/155 g)
1–2 tablespoons paprika, depending on taste
1/2 teaspoon salt, or to taste
Freshly ground pepper (optional)
Chopped fresh parsley

★ Core and peel the tomatoes (see page 123). Cut in half crosswise and squeeze out the seeds. Chop coarsely; you should have 2–2 1/2 cups (12–15 oz/375–470 g). Set aside.

★ Trim any excess fat from the veal cubes. In a large, heavy sauté pan (preferably nonstick) over medium heat, warm the 2 tablespoons oil. When hot, add the veal pieces in batches and sauté gently until lightly seared on all sides, 3–4 minutes; do not allow to brown. Transfer to a plate and set aside.

★ Add the onion to the same pan over medium-low heat, adding more oil if needed to prevent scorching, and sauté gently, stirring, until translucent, about 3 minutes. Add the tomatoes, bell pepper, paprika, and salt and cook, stirring occasionally, for another few minutes.

★ Return the veal to the pan and let cook, uncovered, over medium-low heat until the veal is tender and the sauce thickens, 50–60 minutes or longer. Stir gently every now and again to prevent sticking; add a little water, if needed, to keep the meat from burning.

★ Season to taste with pepper, if desired, then taste and adjust the seasonings. Serve garnished with parsley.

NOTES

This simple stew relies on the complementary flavors of tomatoes, onions, green bell peppers, and paprika to enrobe cubes of delicate veal. Serve it with egg noodles or rice.

The sweet pepper paprika, was one of the vegetables transported by Columbus from the New World to Spain. It flourished there and eventually made its way to Hungary, where it became a cornerstone of the cuisine. Early Eastern European settlers in North America brought the pepper back to its home hemisphere, where paprika has become a favorite spice. I prefer the Hungarian paprika; whatever paprika you use, however, must be absolutely fresh, since the flavor of the powdered spice diminishes quickly.

Be sure to sear the veal without browning it. The ultimate success of the dish lies in the slow cooking and natural thickening of its sauce, so care should be taken that the heat stays low and that you stir regularly to prevent sticking or burning.

SERVES 4

Corned Beef and Vegetables

1 corned center-cut brisket or top round of beef, 3^{1}/$_{2}$–4 lb (1.75–2 kg)

2 celery stalks, cut into pieces

1 large carrot, peeled and cut in half

1 large yellow onion, quartered

3 whole cloves

4 or 5 fresh thyme sprigs

1 large bay leaf

^{1}/$_{8}$ teaspoon red pepper flakes

3 orange zest strips, each 3 inches (7.5 cm) long by 1 inch (2.5 cm) wide
   (see page 122)

4 or 5 large fresh parsley sprigs

6 white potatoes (about 2 lb/1 kg)

6 young turnips or small rutabagas (about 2 lb/1 kg)

1 small head cabbage

★ Rinse the corned beef well, put into a large bowl with water to cover, and let soak for 1 hour to remove some of the brine.

★ Drain the beef, rinse again, and put into a large, heavy pot or Dutch oven in which it fits comfortably. Add water to cover by 1 inch (2.5 cm). Bring to a boil and, using a skimmer or kitchen spoon, skim off the scum from the surface. Reduce the heat so that the water just simmers and add the celery, carrot, onion, cloves, thyme, bay leaf, red pepper flakes, orange zest strips, and parsley. Cover with the lid slightly ajar and simmer over low heat until tender, 2^{1}/$_{2}$–3 hours, adding water as needed to maintain original level. To test for doneness, insert a sharp 2-prong fork in the meat; it should go in easily. Do not overcook, however, or the meat will be dry and stringy.

★ While the corned beef cooks, peel the potatoes and the turnips or rutabagas and cut in half or into quarters. Put the vegetables into a large bowl and add water to cover; set aside. Remove any bruised or old leaves from the cabbage and cut the head into 6 or 8 wedges. Put into a plastic bag and set aside.

★ About 25 minutes before the meat is done, add the potatoes to the pot, let cook for 10 minutes, then add the turnips or rutabagas. Test the meat and vegetables for doneness by piercing with a fork. When tender, transfer to a plate, cover with aluminum foil, and keep warm. Turn up the heat, add the cabbage, and boil until tender, about 5 minutes. Transfer to the plate holding the other vegetables.

★ Slice the meat thinly across the grain and arrange on a serving platter. Surround with the vegetables and serve.

NOTES

Of all the long-cooked meats, corned beef is probably the most practical and versatile. It is delicious hot or cold, and the leftovers are always excellent. Cooking corned beef on a weekend provides a great Sunday family supper, plus other easy meals during the week, including Corned Beef Hash with Poached Eggs (recipe on page 61) or sliced corned beef sandwiches with mustard on a good delicatessen rye bread.

Buy your corned beef from a reliable butcher —preferably one that corns its own beef. (The word corn refers to the kernels of coarse salt used in the meat's preserving process.) Kosher butcher shops are often good sources. Select a high-quality cut such as center-cut brisket or top round.

Have a selection of good mustards on hand to offer with the meat, or serve it with Roasted Red Pepper Sauce (page 120) with 1 teaspoon mustard or prepared horseradish added to it.

SERVES 4
WITH LEFTOVERS

Sautéed Pork Tenderloin with Gingered Apples

1 lb (500 g) tart apples such as Granny Smith
4 tablespoons (2 oz/60 g) unsalted butter
2 tablespoons light brown sugar
1 teaspoon peeled and grated fresh ginger
2–4 tablespoons water
8 slices pork tenderloin, each 3–3 1/2 oz (90–105 g) and about 2 inches (5 cm) thick
Salt and freshly ground pepper
1 tablespoon extra-virgin olive oil or vegetable oil
Small fresh mint sprigs

★ Peel, quarter, and core the apples, then thinly slice lengthwise. In a heavy sauté pan or frying pan over medium heat, melt 3 tablespoons of the butter. When hot, add the apples and sauté, stirring and tossing, for 5 minutes. Add the brown sugar and ginger and continue to sauté, stirring, for another 5 minutes. Add 2 tablespoons of the water, cover, reduce the heat, and cook until the apples are almost tender, 6–8 minutes; watch carefully so they do not burn. Set aside.

★ Trim all excess fat from the pork slices. Place each pork slice, cut side up, between 2 sheets of plastic wrap and, using a rolling pin, flatten to about 1 inch (2.5 cm) thickness. Sprinkle both sides with salt and pepper.

★ In a large sauté pan or frying pan (preferably nonstick) over medium-high heat, melt the remaining 1 tablespoon butter with the oil. When hot, add the pork slices, 4 at a time, and sauté, turning once or twice, until browned and no longer pink at the center, 4–5 minutes on each side. Transfer to a warmed plate; keep warm.

★ When all the pork slices are cooked, pour off the fat from the pan and return to medium heat. Add the apples and their juices and stir to loosen any browned bits on the bottom. Add the remaining 1–2 tablespoons water if there is too little liquid in the pan or the apples are sticking. Sauté the apples until well heated, 2–3 minutes. Return the pork slices and their juices to the pan and heat on each side for a few seconds.

★ Arrange the pork slices on a warmed serving platter or on individual plates and top with the apple slices. Garnish with the mint.

Lamb Stew with Raisins

2 lb (1 kg) boneless lamb shoulder, cut into 1-inch (2.5-cm) cubes

1/2 cup (2¹/2 oz/75 g) all-purpose (plain) flour

3 tablespoons extra-virgin olive oil or vegetable oil

2 cloves garlic, chopped (1 tablespoon)

1/2 teaspoon ground cumin

1/2 teaspoon ground coriander

1 teaspoon ground cinnamon

Pinch of cayenne pepper

1 bay leaf

1¹/2 cups (12 fl oz/375 ml) hot tap water

2 leeks

3 or 4 carrots, peeled and thinly sliced (1¹/2 cups/6 oz/185 g)

1/2 cup (3 oz/90 g) golden raisins (sultanas)

1 teaspoon salt, or to taste

Freshly ground pepper

1 lemon

NOTES

A traditional stew that reflects the blending of cultures in American cooking, this dish takes its seasoning from the kitchens of North Africa. I have used leeks in place of the onions one might expect in such a stew; they add an extra edge of sweetness that, along with the raisins, complements the lamb. The stew can be served with rice or noodles.

Feel free to taste and adjust any of the strong spices to suit your taste. It is important to let the spices cook in the oil for a few minutes to bring out their flavor before you add liquid.

SERVES 4

★ Remove all excess fat from the lamb pieces. Put the flour on a plate. Toss the lamb in the flour to coat lightly, then shake off any excess. In a large, heavy pot or sauté pan over medium-high heat, warm the oil. When hot, add the lamb cubes in batches and lightly brown on all sides, 5–6 minutes. Transfer to a plate and set aside.

★ Add the garlic to the same pan over low heat, stir for a few seconds, then stir in the cumin, coriander, cinnamon, cayenne pepper, and bay leaf and cook for 1–2 minutes. Add the hot water and stir to scrape up any browned bits. Return the meat to the pan and simmer, stirring, until the liquid thickens, about 2 minutes. Cover and simmer over low heat, stirring every now and then, for 1 hour.

★ Meanwhile, trim the leeks, leaving some tender green tops intact. Cut a length-wise slit along each leek to within 2 inches (5 cm) of the root end. Hold under running water to wash away any dirt lodged in the leaves. Cut into slices 1/2 inch (12 mm) thick; you should have about 2 cups (8 oz/250 g). Set aside.

★ At the end of the 1-hour cooking time, blanch the leeks: Bring a saucepan three-fourths full of water to a boil, add the leeks and boil for 2 minutes. Drain and add to the lamb along with the carrots, raisins, salt, and pepper to taste. Simmer, covered, until the meat is tender when pierced with a fork, 40–50 minutes longer. Taste and adjust the seasonings.

★ Transfer the stew to a warmed serving dish. Using a zester or fine-holed shredder, and holding the lemon over the stew, shred the zest from the lemon as directed on page 122. Serve at once.

Meat Loaf with Red Pepper Sauce

1 lb (500 g) ground (minced) lean beef (top or bottom round or sirloin)

$^1/2$ lb (250 g) ground (minced) veal

$^1/2$ lb (250 g) ground (minced) pork

2 tablespoons extra-virgin olive oil or vegetable oil

1 yellow onion, chopped (1 cup/4 oz/125 g)

1 celery stalk, chopped ($^1/2$ cup/$2^1/2$ oz/75 g)

$^1/2$ red bell pepper (capsicum), seeded, deribbed, and chopped ($^1/2$ cup/$2^1/2$ oz/75 g)

1 teaspoon minced fresh oregano

3 or 4 slices French or Italian bread, preferably day-old

$^1/3$ cup (3 fl oz/80 ml) milk

1 egg, lightly beaten

2 teaspoons salt

Freshly ground pepper

$^1/4$ cup (2 fl oz/60 ml) dry red wine, or as needed

Roasted Red Pepper Sauce (recipe on page 120)

(recipe on page 120)

★ Position a rack in the middle of an oven and preheat the oven to 375°F (190°C). Grease a $1^1/2$- or 2-qt (1.5- or 2-l) baking dish or baking pan. In a large bowl, combine the beef, veal, and pork. Mix lightly. Set aside.

★ In a sauté pan over medium-low heat, warm the oil. Add the onion and sauté for 1 minute. Stir in the celery, bell pepper, and oregano. Cover and cook over low heat, stirring a couple of times, until tender, 4–5 minutes; do not brown.

★ Remove the crusts from the bread. Cut or tear the bread into small pieces and put into a food processor fitted with the metal blade or into a blender. Pulse to make coarse crumbs (2 cups/4 oz/125 g). Transfer to a small bowl. Stirring with a fork, dribble the milk onto the crumbs. Let stand a few minutes.

★ To the bowl holding the meat add the onion mixture, bread crumbs, egg, salt, and pepper to taste. Using your hands, mix well. Form into a loaf (do not pack too solidly) and place in the baking dish or pan. Pour the wine over the meat.

★ Bake uncovered, basting every 15 minutes with the pan juices, until cooked through, about $1^1/2$ hours; add more wine to the dish if it begins to dry out. To test for doneness, insert an instant-read thermometer into the center of the meat loaf; it should read 165°F (74°C). Remove from the oven and cover loosely with foil; let rest for 5–10 minutes.

★ Slice thinly and spoon a little of the Roasted Red Pepper Sauce over the slices.

NOTES

Excellent served hot, this meat loaf can yield leftovers; serve them cold with salad as a main course, in sandwiches, or even chopped and added to a tomato sauce for pasta.

Once you mix the meats together, let the mixture come to room temperature. The meat is seasoned with fresh oregano, but you can substitute $^1/2$ teaspoon dried oregano if fresh is unavailable. Be sure to crush it in the palm of your hand with your thumb before using.

SERVES 4–6

Corned Beef Hash
with Poached Eggs

2 baking potatoes, about 1½ lb (750 g) total weight, unpeeled

1½ teaspoons salt, plus salt to taste

5 tablespoons (2½ oz/75 g) unsalted butter

1 yellow onion, diced (1 cup/4 oz/125 g)

1 red or green bell pepper (capsicum), seeded, deribbed, and diced
 (1 cup/5 oz/155 g)

1 celery stalk, diced (½ cup/2½ oz/75 g)

1 teaspoon chopped fresh oregano or ½ teaspoon dried oregano

3 cups (about 1 lb/500 g) diced, chopped, or shredded cooked corned beef

4 tablespoons chopped fresh parsley, plus extra for garnish

Freshly ground pepper

2–3 tablespoons white cider vinegar

4 or 8 very fresh extra-large or jumbo eggs

★ In a saucepan, combine the potatoes and 1 teaspoon of the salt with water to cover. Bring to a boil, cover partially, and boil until slightly underdone, 15–20 minutes. Drain and set aside until cool enough to handle.

★ In a large sauté pan over medium-low heat, melt 2 tablespoons of the butter. Add the onion and sauté until almost translucent, 2–3 minutes. Add the bell pepper, celery, and oregano; cover and cook over low heat, stirring occasionally, until soft, 8–10 minutes. Set aside.

★ Peel and cut the potatoes into ½-inch (12-mm) dice. In a large sauté pan over medium heat, melt the remaining 3 tablespoons butter. Add the potatoes and sauté for 5–6 minutes. Mix in the onion-pepper mixture, corned beef, the 4 tablespoons parsley, and pepper to taste. Cover and cook until heated through, 2–3 minutes. Season to taste with salt and pepper. Cover and keep warm.

★ To poach the eggs, in a large sauté pan, pour in water to a depth of 1½ inches (4 cm). Add the vinegar and the remaining ½ teaspoon salt and bring to a boil. Reduce the heat so that the liquid is just under a boil. Break an egg into a saucer and gently slip the egg into the water. Repeat with the other eggs, spacing well apart. Cook in the hot water until the whites are firm and the yolks are glazed over but still liquid, 3–5 minutes. Remove the eggs with a skimmer or a large slotted spoon, allowing them to drain, and place on a flat plate. Trim the edges of whites if they are ragged.

★ Arrange the hash on a warmed platter and top with the eggs, or serve the hash and eggs on individual plates. Garnish with chopped parsley.

NOTES

Since the nineteenth century, corned beef hash has been a staple on the breakfast menus of cafés and restaurants across the United States: Nothing could be more American. In fact, cafés known for their corned beef hash affectionately became known as hash houses. Use the leftovers from your corned beef dinner (recipe on page 53) for making the hash. Then all you need is a simple green salad to round out the menu for a delightful weekend brunch or supper. Try serving the hash with Roasted Red Pepper Sauce (page 120) with 1 teaspoon of prepared horseradish added to it.

A few insider's secrets and a little practice will ensure perfect poached eggs for serving on top of your hash. Start with very fresh eggs, which have the firmest whites and yolks. A splash of vinegar in the poaching water helps firm up the whites quickly. And swirling the water while gently lowering the egg into the vortex of the swirl will prevent the white from spreading out in the water.

SERVES 4

Broiled Swordfish Steaks with Basil, Olive Oil, and Capers

4 tablespoons (2 fl oz/60 ml) fresh lemon juice
Salt and freshly ground pepper
1/2 cup (4 fl oz/120 ml) extra-virgin olive oil
2 tablespoons chopped fresh basil
4 swordfish steaks, 7–8 oz (220–250 g) each, 3/4–1 inch (2–2.5 cm) thick
1/4 cup (3/4 oz/20 g) minced green (spring) onion, including some tender green tops
1/4 cup (2 oz/60 g) well-drained capers, rinsed

★ Preheat a broiler (griller).

★ In a small bowl, combine 1 tablespoon of the lemon juice and 1 or 2 pinches each of salt and pepper and stir until the salt dissolves. Add 1/4 cup (2 fl oz/60 ml) of the olive oil and 1 tablespoon of the basil; stir well. Rinse the swordfish steaks and pat dry with paper towels. Brush both sides of each fish steak with some of the mixture and place on the rack of a broiler pan.

★ Place under the broiler about 2 inches (5 cm) from the heat source. Broil (grill), basting with the remaining olive oil mixture a couple of times, until the fish is opaque throughout when pierced with a sharp knife, 5–6 minutes on each side.

★ Meanwhile, in a small bowl, combine the remaining 3 tablespoons lemon juice and 1 or 2 pinches each of salt and pepper; stir until the salt dissolves. Add the remaining 1/4 cup (2 fl oz/60 ml) olive oil, the remaining 1 tablespoon basil, the green onion, and capers. Stir to mix well.

★ When the fish steaks are done, transfer to warmed plates and spoon the olive oil–caper sauce over the fish. Pass any remaining sauce in a bowl at the table.

NOTES

Satisfyingly meaty and yet mild in flavor, swordfish is caught along both the Atlantic and Pacific coasts and is available almost everywhere. Usually cooked by broiling, the dense flesh requires frequent basting to keep it from becoming dry; care must also be taken not to overcook it.

Prepare the sauce in advance so that you can serve the fish immediately. If fresh basil is unavailable, don't use dried, which doesn't approach the flavor of the fresh herb; instead, substitute about 1 teaspoon fresh or dried dill. Crush the dried herb in the palm of your hand with your thumb before adding it.

SERVES 4

Spanish Rice with Shrimp

³/₄–1 lb (375–500 g) small or medium shrimp (prawns) in the shell
Salt
1¹/₂ lb (750 g) ripe plum (Roma) tomatoes
4 tablespoons (2 fl oz/60 ml) extra-virgin olive oil, or as needed
3 oz (90 g) cooked ham, cut into small strips (³/₄ cup)
2 or 3 cloves garlic, depending upon your taste and size of cloves, minced
1 yellow onion, diced (1 cup/4 oz/125 g)
1 celery stalk, diced (¹/₂ cup/2¹/₂ oz/75 g)
1 green bell pepper (capsicum), seeded, deribbed, and diced (1 cup/5 oz/155 g)
1 cup (8 fl oz/250 ml) water
Pinch of cayenne pepper
1 cup (7 oz/220 g) medium-grain white rice
Chopped fresh flat-leaf (Italian) parsley or regular parsley
Lemon wedges *(optional)*

★ Position a rack in the middle of an oven and preheat the oven to 350°F (180°C). Butter a shallow 2-qt (2-l) baking dish.

★ Peel and devein the shrimp *(see page 123)*. Put the shrimp in a bowl with water to cover. Add 1 teaspoon salt, stir to dissolve, and let stand for 10 minutes to freshen the shrimp. Drain, rinse, and drain again. Set aside.

★ Core, peel, and seed the tomatoes *(see page 123)*. Chop coarsely. Set aside.

★ In a large sauté pan or frying pan over medium-high heat, warm 2 tablespoons of the oil. Add the shrimp and sauté quickly, stirring and tossing, just until they turn pink, about 5 minutes. Transfer to a plate and set aside. Add the ham to the same pan and place over medium-low heat. Adding more oil if needed, sauté, stirring, 2–3 minutes. Then add the garlic and onion and sauté, stirring, until translucent, 3–4 minutes longer. Add the celery, bell pepper, and tomatoes, stir well and cook uncovered, stirring occasionally, until the tomatoes start to break down, another 6–8 minutes. Stir in the water, ¹/₂ teaspoon salt, and the cayenne pepper. Transfer to a bowl and set aside.

★ Heat the remaining 2 tablespoons oil in the same pan over medium heat. Add the rice and cook, stirring, until translucent, 2–3 minutes. Return the tomato mixture to the pan along with the shrimp and cook over low heat, stirring occasionally, about 8 minutes. Taste and adjust the seasonings.

★ Transfer the rice mixture to the prepared baking dish, cover loosely with aluminum foil, and bake for 15 minutes. Remove the foil and continue to bake until the rice is just tender, another 10–15 minutes.

★ Remove from the oven, re-cover with the foil, and let stand for 10 minutes. Garnish with parsley and serve. Pass a bowl of lemon wedges, if desired.

NOTES

I suppose Spanish rice had its beginning in the American Southwest. Certainly by the first half of the 20th century it was popular throughout the United States. I like to think of this as a simple paella: The shrimp, ham, and bell pepper transform it into a one-dish meal.

If you'd like a little more spice in your rice, add 1 or 2 mild fresh chile peppers, seeded and chopped, with the garlic and onion.

SERVES 4

Poached Salmon Steaks with Cucumbers

2 cucumbers

Salt

1/3 cup (3 fl oz/80 ml) sour cream

2 teaspoons minced fresh dill

4 cups (32 fl oz/1 l) water

1/2 cup (4 fl oz/125 ml) dry white wine

1/2 celery stalk, cut into chunks

1 carrot, cut into chunks

1/4 yellow onion, cut into chunks

2 thin lemon slices, plus 1 lemon, cut into wedges, for garnish

4 peppercorns

3 fresh parsley sprigs

1 bay leaf

4 salmon steaks, 6–8 oz (185–250 g) each

★ Peel the cucumbers and cut in half lengthwise. Using a melon baller or a small spoon, scoop out the seeds and discard. Cut crosswise into slices 1/4 inch (6 mm) thick. In a colander set over a bowl, layer half of the cucumber slices. Sprinkle with salt, then top with the remaining cucumber slices and again sprinkle with salt. Rest a small plate directly on the cucumbers; weight down the plate with a couple of food tins. Leave to drain in the refrigerator for 2–2 1/2 hours. Dry the cucumber slices with paper towels and return them to the refrigerator.

★ In a small bowl, stir together the sour cream and dill. Cover and refrigerate.

★ In a large sauté pan or roasting pan with high sides that will hold the salmon steaks in one layer without crowding, combine the water, wine, celery, carrot, onion, 2 lemon slices, peppercorns, parsley, bay leaf, and 2 teaspoons salt. Bring to a simmer, cover, and simmer over low heat for 25–30 minutes.

★ Rinse the salmon steaks. Using kitchen string, tie each steak to hold its shape. Add the steaks to the simmering liquid, cover or partially cover, and simmer gently over low heat for 10 minutes. Check for doneness by inserting a knife into the salmon; the flesh should be opaque throughout. Do not overcook.

★ Just before serving, again dry the cucumber slices, then combine them with the sour cream mixture in a bowl. Mix until well blended.

★ Using a spatula, transfer the salmon pieces to individual plates. Add 1 or 2 spoonfuls of the cucumber mixture and a lemon wedge to each plate. Serve at once.

Fillets of Sole with Mustard-Horseradish Sauce

NOTES

Sole has a wonderfully delicate texture, but it can also be fairly bland. I've found that the fish stands up well to stronger seasonings, such as the mustard and horseradish used here. Other mild-flavored whitefish—sea bass, halibut, red snapper—can also be prepared this way.

Just a few ingredients go into the dish, but all of them play key roles, so pay close attention to their quality. Seek out mushrooms that are small and firm, without the brown filaments on the undersides of the caps that indicate they are old. Make your own fresh bread crumbs from an Italian or French loaf. Use freshly grated Parmesan cheese, preferably Parmegiano-Reggiano. And the plain prepared horseradish found in the refrigerated section of your food store will have a far superior flavor to the one found bottled in the condiments aisle.

SERVES 4

2 or 3 slices French or Italian bread
$1/2$ lb (250 g) small fresh mushrooms
$1/4$ cup (2 oz/60 g) unsalted butter
1 large or 2 small shallots, chopped (2 tablespoons)
Juice of 1 lemon (about 3 tablespoons)
3–4 tablespoons Dijon mustard
$1–1^{1}/_{2}$ tablespoons prepared horseradish
$1/4$ cup (1 oz/30 g) freshly grated Parmesan cheese
$1/2$ cup (4 fl oz/125 ml) sour cream
Salt and freshly ground pepper
4 sole fillets, 6–7 oz (185–220 g) each

★ Position a rack in the lower part of an oven and preheat the oven to 425°F (220°C). Butter a flameproof baking dish that will accommodate the fish fillets in a single layer without crowding.

★ Remove the crusts from the bread and discard. Cut or tear the bread into small pieces and put into a food processor fitted with the metal blade or into a blender. Pulse a few times to make coarse crumbs; you should have $1–1^{1}/_{2}$ cups (2–$2^{1}/_{2}$ oz/60–75 g). Set aside.

★ Clean the mushrooms by brushing them with a soft-bristled brush or a paper towel; do not wash. Slice thinly and set aside.

★ In a sauté pan over medium-low heat, melt the butter. Add the shallots and sauté, stirring, for 1 minute. Raise the heat to medium, add the mushrooms, and cook, stirring and tossing, until the mushrooms are just wilted, 2–3 minutes. Set aside.

★ In a bowl, stir together the lemon juice, mustard, horseradish, Parmesan cheese, and sour cream until well blended. Add to the mushrooms, return to the heat, and bring just to a simmer. Stir to blend and season to taste with salt and pepper.

★ Rinse the sole fillets and pat dry with paper towels. Place in the prepared baking dish in a single layer and spoon the sauce over the fillets. Sprinkle the bread crumbs evenly over the top. Bake until the fish is opaque throughout when pierced with a sharp knife, 10–20 minutes; the timing depends upon the thickness of the fillets.

★ Preheat a broiler (griller). Slip the baking dish under the broiler and broil (grill) to brown the top lightly, 1–2 minutes. Serve at once.

Baked Shrimp with Dill

1 lb (500 g) medium shrimp (prawns) in the shell (about 24)

1¹/₈ teaspoons salt

1 or 2 cloves garlic, depending upon taste and size of cloves, minced

2 tablespoons minced green (spring) onion, including some tender green tops

2 tablespoons chopped fresh parsley

1 tablespoon chopped fresh dill

2 tablespoons fresh lime juice

Freshly ground pepper

3–4 tablespoons extra-virgin olive oil

★ Position a rack in the middle of an oven and preheat to 450°F (230°C). Oil a large, shallow baking dish, preferably a round dish 10 inches (25 cm) in diameter.

★ Peel, devein, and butterfly the shrimp *(see page 123)*. Place the shrimp in a bowl and add water to cover. Add 1 teaspoon of the salt, stir to dissolve, and let stand for 10 minutes. Drain, rinse, and drain again; dry on paper towels. Arrange the shrimp in the prepared baking dish, placing them close together in concentric circles and with cut part down and spread out and tails up.

★ Sprinkle the garlic, green onion, parsley, and dill evenly over the shrimp. In a small bowl, stir together the lime juice, the remaining ¹/₈ teaspoon salt, and pepper to taste, mixing well to dissolve the salt. Whisk in the olive oil and sprinkle evenly over the shrimp.

★ Bake until the shrimp are pink, 8–10 minutes. Do not overbake or they will toughen. Serve at once.

NOTES

As most raw shrimp available in fish markets were flash-frozen at the time of the catch, I prefer to soak them in salted water for 10–15 minutes to freshen them and rid them of any odor. After soaking, rinse well in fresh water before use. Butterflying the shrimp not only makes a more attractive presentation but also helps to cook them faster. Serve with a good crusty French or Italian bread, adding a green salad to make a good weekend lunch or supper.

If fresh dill is unavailable, use 1–2 teaspoons dried, placing the herb in the palm of one hand and using the thumb of the other to crush it, to release all the flavor. If you like the flavor of dill, feel free to increase the measure.

SERVES 4

Crab Cakes

3 or 4 slices French or Italian bread

3 tablespoons unsalted butter

1/4 cup (1 oz/30 g) minced green (spring) onion, including some
   tender green tops (3 or 4 onions)

1 lb (500 g) fresh cooked crab meat, picked over to remove any
   shell fragments and cartilage

1 tablespoon chopped fresh parsley

1/3 cup (3 fl oz/80 ml) heavy (double) cream

2 eggs

2 tablespoons fresh lemon juice

1 tablespoon Dijon mustard

1/2 teaspoon salt, or to taste

Cayenne pepper

1/2 cup (2 1/2 oz/75 g) all-purpose (plain) flour

2 tablespoons vegetable oil

Lemon wedges

★ Remove the crusts from the bread and discard. Cut or tear the bread into small
pieces and put into a food processor fitted with the metal blade or into a blender.
Pulse a few times to make coarse crumbs; you should have about 2 cups (4 oz/125 g). Place
in a large bowl and set aside.

★ In a small sauté pan over low heat, melt 1 tablespoon of the butter. Add the onion
and sauté until softened, 1–2 minutes. Add the onion to the bread crumbs along with
the crab meat and parsley. Mix well.

★ In a separate bowl, whisk together the cream and eggs until well blended. Whisk
in the lemon juice, mustard, salt, and cayenne pepper to taste. Slowly add to the crab
mixture, stirring continuously so that the bread crumbs are evenly moistened. Taste
and adjust the seasonings.

★ Form into 8 or 12 oval or round cakes about 1 inch (2.5 cm) thick. Put the flour on
a plate or on a piece of waxed paper. Lightly and evenly coat each patty with the
flour, shaking off any excess.

★ In a large sauté pan or frying pan over medium-high heat, melt the remaining
2 tablespoons butter with the vegetable oil. When hot, sauté the cakes in batches,
turning once, until lightly browned, 3–4 minutes on each side. Transfer to a warmed
plate and keep warm until all the cakes are cooked.

★ Serve immediately with lemon wedges.

NOTES

Crab cakes are a permanent fixture
in the cooking of America's eastern
seaboard from the New England
states to Georgia. An abundance
of recipes from Baltimore and the
Chesapeake Bay, Virginia, and
elsewhere along the East Coast,
each different from the others, all
claim to be the most authentic.

The key to successful crab cakes lies
in using fresh cooked crab meat and
lots of it, with just a little something
extra to bind the mixture. The distri-
bution of fresh crab has improved in
recent years, and you can find it in
good seafood markets all through the
winter and spring. Most recipes use
mayonnaise as a binder; I prefer to
use cream mixed with egg and
seasoned with fresh lemon juice,
mustard, and cayenne pepper. A
small amount of bread crumbs also
helps lighten and bind the mixture;
be sure to use your own freshly made
crumbs from French or Italian bread.

SERVES 4

Baked Sea Bass with Tomato and Fennel

2 or 3 slices French or Italian bread

1¹/₂ lb (750 g) ripe plum (Roma) tomatoes

4 tablespoons (2 oz/60 g) unsalted butter

1 small yellow onion, diced (¹/₂ cup/2 oz/60 g)

Salt and freshly ground pepper

1 fennel bulb, about 1 lb (500 g)

2 tablespoons water

4 sea bass fillets, about 6–8 oz (185–250 g) each

1 lemon, cut in half, plus 1 whole lemon

1 tablespoon fennel seeds

★ Position a rack in the lower part of an oven and preheat to 425°F (220°C). Butter a flameproof baking dish that will hold the fish fillets in one layer.

★ Remove the crusts from the bread. Cut the bread into small pieces and put into a food processor fitted with the metal blade or into a blender. Pulse a few times to make coarse crumbs (1–1¹/₂ cups/2–2¹/₂ oz/60–75 g). Set aside.

★ Core, peel, and seed the tomatoes (see page 123). Chop coarsely. In a saucepan over medium-low heat, melt 2 tablespoons of the butter. Add the onion and sauté until translucent. Add the tomatoes, raise the heat to medium, and cook, stirring, until softened, 3–4 minutes longer. Season to taste with salt and pepper; set aside.

★ Trim off any stems and bruised stalks from the fennel. Thinly slice the bulb vertically, then cut vertically into thin strips. In a saucepan over low heat, melt the remaining butter. Add the fennel, a pinch of salt, and the water. Cover and cook over low heat until just tender, 10–15 minutes; do not allow to become dry. Uncover, raise the heat, and cook away most of the liquid. Let cool slightly.

★ Scatter half of the fennel in the prepared dish. Rinse and dry the fish fillets. Using 1 lemon half, squeeze juice on both sides of each fillet, sprinkle with salt and pepper, and place atop the fennel. Distribute the remaining fennel over the fillets. Spoon on the tomato mixture and sprinkle with the bread crumbs. Squeeze the other lemon half over the top and scatter on the fennel seeds.

★ Bake, uncovered, until the fish is opaque throughout when pierced with a knife, 15–20 minutes; the timing depends upon the thickness of the fish.

★ Preheat a broiler (griller). Slip the baking dish under the broiler and broil (grill) until lightly browned, 1–2 minutes. Shred the zest from the remaining whole lemon (see page 122), distributing it evenly over the fish. Serve immediately.

NOTES

We can probably thank Italian immigrants for contributing the great combination of fish, fennel, and tomatoes to American kitchens. Covered with the vegetable mixture, the fish bakes to moist perfection. This recipe gets its delicate anise flavor from two different fennel sources—the fresh bulb and the dried seeds of another fennel variety.

Any other whitefish, such as halibut or red snapper, can be substituted for the sea bass, but do not use an oily fish. Take a few moments to run your fingertips over the fillets; pull out any remaining little bones you detect, using tweezers if necessary. You can also use 1 large piece of fish weighing about 1¹/₂ pounds (750 g) instead of the fillets.

SERVES 4

Sautéed Scallops with Spinach

1–2 bunches spinach, 1–1¹/₂ lb (500–750 g)
¹/₂ lb (250 g) ripe plum (Roma) tomatoes
3 tablespoons unsalted butter
2 tablespoons minced shallot
Salt and freshly ground pepper
Pinch of freshly grated nutmeg
1 lb (500 g) sea scallops, cut in half horizontally if large
1 tablespoon extra-virgin olive oil
1–2 tablespoons Madeira, Marsala, or port wine
Lemon wedges

★ Pick over the spinach, discarding any old leaves, and remove the stems. Wash well and put into a bowl with a little water. Set aside.

★ Core, peel, and seed the tomatoes *(see page 123)*. Finely chop; you should have about 1 cup (6 oz/185 g). Set aside.

★ In a saucepan over medium-low heat, melt 1 tablespoon of the butter. Add the shallot and sauté, stirring, until translucent, 1–2 minutes. Add the tomatoes, raise the heat to medium-high, and cook rapidly, stirring, until thickened, 8–10 minutes. Season to taste with salt and pepper. Set aside and cover to keep warm.

★ Transfer the spinach to a large saucepan with just the water clinging to the leaves. Sprinkle with a little salt and the nutmeg, cover, and place over medium-high heat. Cook, turning the leaves over once or twice so they cook evenly, until just wilted, 2–3 minutes. Immediately drain in a colander and press out the water with the back of a wooden spoon. Fluff up the leaves with a fork. Set aside and cover to keep warm.

★ Rinse the scallops and dry with paper towels. In a large sauté pan or frying pan (preferably nonstick) over medium-high heat, melt the remaining 2 tablespoons butter with the olive oil. When bubbling, add the scallops in batches and sauté, turning once, until beginning to brown, 1–2 minutes on each side. Transfer to a warmed plate and keep warm. Add the tomatoes to the pan and heat to a simmer. Stir in the Madeira or other wine; taste and adjust the seasonings. Return the scallops to the pan and heat through to serving temperature.

★ Arrange the spinach around the perimeter of a warmed serving dish. Spoon the scallops and tomato sauce into the center. Garnish with lemon wedges.

NOTES

Scallops and spinach are a classic combination of tastes, textures, and colors—an ideal light main course for lunch or supper.

Buy your scallops from a reliable seafood market. I find large sea scallops easier to sauté, but use the smaller bay scallops if you prefer. If the sea scallops that you purchase are very large or thick, slice them in half horizontally to make two thinner rounds from each scallop. They'll take only 1–2 minutes to cook on each side. Be careful not to overcook them, as they quickly lose their delicate tenderness. The scallops are ready just at the moment they turn opaque and are lightly tinged with brown.

SERVES 4

Cauliflower with Cherry Tomatoes

1 head of cauliflower, about 2 lb (1 kg)

1 fresh green Anaheim chile pepper or Hungarian wax pepper

3/4 lb (375 g) small ripe cherry tomatoes (about 2 cups)

2 tablespoons unsalted butter

1/2 yellow onion, chopped (1/2 cup/2 oz/60 g)

2 tablespoons water

2 teaspoons chopped fresh cilantro (fresh coriander)

Salt and freshly ground pepper

★ Remove the florets from the head of cauliflower. Cut any large ones in half, so they are all the same size. Set aside.

★ Slice the pepper in half lengthwise. Remove the seeds and ribs and discard. Cut crosswise into slices 1/8 inch (3 mm) thick. Set aside.

★ Remove the stems from the cherry tomatoes. Slice one-third of the tomatoes in half and leave the remainder whole. Set aside.

★ Bring a saucepan three-fourths full of water to a boil. Add the cauliflower and bring back to a boil. Reduce the heat to medium and cook, uncovered, at a gentle boil until just tender but still crisp, 5–6 minutes. Drain and keep warm. Alternatively, put the cauliflower in a steamer basket and place in a saucepan over simmering water. Cover and steam until tender, 6–7 minutes. Set aside.

★ Meanwhile, in a sauté pan over medium-low heat, melt the butter. Add the onion and sauté, stirring, for 1 minute. Add 1 tablespoon of the water, cover, and cook, stirring occasionally, until translucent, 3–4 minutes. Add the pepper slices and the remaining 1 tablespoon water, cover, and cook, stirring occasionally, for another 3–4 minutes. Uncover, add all the tomatoes, 1/2 teaspoon of the cilantro, and salt and pepper to taste. Sauté uncovered, stirring and tossing, until the halved tomatoes begin to break down and release their juices, 1–2 minutes. Taste and adjust the seasonings. Remove from the heat.

★ Arrange the cauliflower in a serving dish and spoon the tomato mixture over it. Sprinkle with the remaining 1 1/2 teaspoons cilantro.

NOTES

American cooking has gradually absorbed the spices and herbs of many other cuisines, enhancing even the simplest preparations of vegetables and meats. The mild Anaheim (New Mexican) chile pepper, or the Hungarian wax variety, goes well with some of our blander vegetables, like the cauliflower in this recipe. Cilantro, too, adds bright, fresh flavor to this dish. Small, sweet cherry tomatoes are also the perfect companion in both taste and color.

SERVES 4

Macaroni and Cheese with Broccoli

NOTES

For some reason or other, even though pasta has become a favorite in recent years, we have forgotten how good America's own pasta dish, macaroni and cheese, can be. With a few innovations, macaroni and cheese can stand up to many of the most popular pasta dishes. It enjoys the distinct advantage of advance preparation, making it a great informal meal, and the leftovers can be reheated successfully. Serve it with a green salad.

When I was a child, we always added other ingredients to our macaroni and cheese. By including broccoli, tomatoes, cauliflower, or leftover chicken, shrimp, or scallops, you can turn this dish into something special.

I've chosen white Cheddar cheese for this recipe because I wanted the sauce to remain white. Use New England white Cheddar, if possible, as it is one of the best natural cheeses made in the United States. Take care not to allow the sauce to become too thick. And use freshly made bread crumbs for the topping.

SERVES 4

2 slices French or Italian bread
1¹/₂ cups (12 fl oz/375 ml) milk
¹/₄ white onion (or 1 small onion) stuck with 2 whole cloves
1 bunch broccoli, about 1¹/₂ lb (750 g)
2 tablespoons unsalted butter
2 tablespoons all-purpose (plain) flour
1¹/₂ cups (6 oz/185 g) shredded aged white Cheddar cheese
Salt and freshly ground pepper, preferably white pepper
Freshly grated nutmeg
2 teaspoons dry sherry
1 cup (3¹/₂ oz/105 g) small elbow macaroni

★ Position a rack in the upper part of an oven and preheat the oven to 325°F (165°C). Butter a shallow 2-qt (2-l) baking dish. Remove the crusts from the bread. Cut the bread into small pieces and put into a food processor fitted with the metal blade or into a blender. Pulse a few times to make coarse crumbs. Set aside.

★ In a saucepan over medium heat, combine the milk and the clove-pierced onion. Warm to a simmer. Remove from the heat; set aside for 10–15 minutes. Meanwhile, cut or break the florets off the broccoli stalks. Peel the stalks and cut into small chunks. Cut any large florets in half. Set aside.

★ In a saucepan over low heat, melt the butter. Using a whisk or wooden spoon, stir in the flour and cook, stirring, for 30–40 seconds; do not brown. Remove from the heat. Using a slotted spoon, remove the onion from the milk and discard. Gradually pour the milk into the flour mixture, stirring briskly. Return to the heat and slowly bring to a boil, continue to stir constantly (scrape the pan bottom and sides to avoid lumping and scorching) until the sauce thickens and is smooth, about 3–4 minutes. Add ¹/₂ cup (2 oz/60 g) of the cheese and stir until blended. Add salt and pepper to taste, a sprinkling of nutmeg, and the sherry.

★ Bring a large pot three-fourths full of water to a boil. Add 1 teaspoon salt and the broccoli. Bring back to a boil and cook until not quite tender, 4–5 minutes. Using a slotted spoon, transfer the broccoli to a colander; immediately place under cold running water to stop the cooking. Drain and set aside. To the still-boiling water, add the macaroni and cook until slightly underdone, 6–8 minutes. Drain well.

★ Place the broccoli in the prepared dish and scatter on the macaroni. Spoon on the sauce, then scatter with the remaining cheese and the bread crumbs. Bake, uncovered, until lightly browned and bubbling, 25–30 minutes. Serve at once.

Leeks in Tomato Sauce

1 lb (500 g) ripe plum (Roma) tomatoes (4 or 5)

4 leeks

1 bay leaf

2 whole cloves

$1/2$ cup (4 fl oz/125 ml) dry white wine, or as needed

$1/2$ cup (4 fl oz/125 ml) chicken stock, or as needed

3 tablespoons extra-virgin olive oil or vegetable oil

$1/4$ cup (1 oz/30 g) diced sweet red (Spanish) onion or other sweet onion

$1/8$ teaspoon salt

Scant $1/4$ teaspoon red pepper flakes

★ Core and peel the tomatoes (see page 123). Cut in half crosswise and carefully squeeze out the seeds. Coarsely chop; you should have about 2 cups (12 oz/375 g). Set aside in a bowl.

★ Trim the leeks, leaving some of the tender green tops intact and cutting them all to the same length. Make a lengthwise slit along each leek to within about 2 inches (5 cm) of the root end. Place under running water to wash away any dirt lodged between the leaves.

★ To blanch the leeks, select a large sauté pan or frying pan that will accommodate the leeks lying flat. Fill three-fourths full of water and bring to a boil. Add the leeks and boil for 2–3 minutes. Drain carefully and, when cool enough to handle, finish cutting the leeks in half lengthwise.

★ In the same pan, place the bay leaf and cloves. Arrange the leek halves on top of the spices in a single layer, cut side up.

★ Add the wine, chicken stock, oil, onion, salt, and red pepper flakes to the bowl holding the tomatoes and stir well to blend. Spoon the tomato mixture evenly over the leeks.

★ Bring the leeks to a simmer, reduce the heat to low, and cook uncovered at a bare simmer (just a few bubbles), basting occasionally, until the leeks are tender, 45–60 minutes; add more chicken stock or wine if too dry.

★ Taste and adjust the seasonings. Serve hot or at room temperature.

NOTES

Try serving this dish hot or at room temperature as a first course, or accompany it with rice to make a light main course. You can also serve the leeks chilled; but in that case you may wish to increase the seasonings slightly, since they will be muted by the cooler temperature.

Easy to prepare, leeks lend themselves well to many recipes. You can substitute them for onions, or include them along with onions, to give a decidedly different flavor. Be sure to rinse the leeks thoroughly to rid them of any sand or grit lodged between the leaves, following the instructions in the recipe.

SERVES 4

Purée of Minted Green Peas

3–4 lb (1.5–2 kg) green peas (amount depends upon fullness of pods)
1 tablespoon unsalted butter
1 white Bermuda onion, coarsely chopped (1 cup/4 oz/125 g)
3 tablespoons water, plus more as needed
$^1/_2$ teaspoon salt
2 teaspoons finely chopped fresh mint
Freshly ground pepper
$^1/_4$ cup (2 fl oz/60 ml) heavy (double) cream

★ Shell the peas. You should have about 4 cups (1$^1/_4$ lb/625 g). Set aside.

★ In a saucepan over medium-low heat, melt the butter. Add the onion and 1 tablespoon of the water, cover tightly, and steam, stirring occasionally, until translucent, about 10 minutes. Do not allow to brown or burn; add more water if necessary.

★ Add the peas, the remaining 2 tablespoons water, and the salt. Raise the heat slightly, cover, and cook, stirring the peas from the bottom every now and again until they are tender and bright green, another 8–10 minutes. The liquid in the pan may increase; but watch that it doesn't boil dry, adding more water if necessary.

★ Drain the peas and onion, reserving the liquid. Put the peas and onion in a food processor fitted with the metal blade. Add the mint, 1 tablespoon of the cooking liquid, and pepper to taste. Process to form a soft purée. Add more cooking liquid if necessary to achieve the correct consistency. Alternatively, pass the mixture through a food mill *(see page 121)*.

★ Return to the pan and stir in the cream. Reheat, while stirring, for a few seconds, until hot. Taste and adjust the seasonings and serve.

NOTES

I'm always looking for new ways to cook peas, especially because they can be so inconsistent in the cooking time they take to reach tenderness. A purée, I have found, irons out those inconsistencies and highlights the sweet flavor of the peas. Another advantage is that you can prepare the purée ahead of time—something you can't really do when you serve whole peas. A small amount of cream enhances the dish's taste; if you prefer, use milk instead.

Pulsing the purée in a food processor gives you fingertip control over its fineness. Alternatively, pass the peas through a food mill *(see page 121)* to get a consistent fine or medium texture, depending on which disk you insert.

SERVES 4

Corn and Green Beans, Circa 1935

4 ears yellow corn, husks and silks removed, trimmed of any defects
$^1/_2$ red bell pepper (capsicum), seeded and deribbed
1 tablespoon unsalted butter
1 slice cooked ham, $^1/_4$ lb (125 g) and $^1/_4$ inch (6 mm) thick, cut into strips
    $1^1/_2$ inches (4 cm) long and $^1/_4$ inch (6 mm) wide
1 or 2 cloves garlic, depending upon your taste and size of cloves, minced
$^1/_2$ lb (250 g) young green beans, trimmed and cut on the diagonal
    into $1^1/_2$-inch (4-cm) lengths
Salt and freshly ground pepper
4 tablespoons (2 fl oz/60 ml) chicken stock or dry white wine, or a mixture,
    plus more as needed

★ Firmly hold each ear of corn, stem end down, on a cutting surface and, using a sharp knife, carefully cut off the kernels; you should have about 3 cups (18 oz/560 g). Set aside.

★ Cut the bell pepper into strips $1^1/_2$ inches (4 cm) long and $^1/_4$ inch (6 mm) wide. Set aside.

★ In a large sauté pan over low heat, melt the butter until it bubbles. When hot, add the ham and garlic and sauté, stirring, 2–3 minutes. Do not allow to brown. Add the corn, green beans, bell pepper, salt and pepper to taste, and 3 tablespoons of the stock and/or wine. Stir to combine, cover tightly, and cook over medium-high heat for 2–3 minutes. Stir and check liquid; add another 1 tablespoon stock and/or wine. Re-cover and cook for another 2–3 minutes. Stir again and, if the pan seems dry, add another 1 tablespoon stock and/or water. Re-cover, cook for 1–2 minutes longer and check doneness of green beans; they should be tender but still crisp and green. If not tender, re-cover and cook longer, adding more stock and/or wine as needed to prevent sticking.

★ Taste and adjust the seasonings. Serve at once.

NOTES

I learned to cook this dish when I was about 17, soon after I moved to California. I suppose it's a variation on the classic American Indian succotash, a mixture of lima beans and corn. In the 1930s, California's kitchens were beginning to change the way Americans cooked, as we all learned about and experimented with an abundance of fresh vegetables. Of course, the tendency then was to cook some of them far too long, green beans being a good example.

I find small, young green beans to be best for this dish; they have a fine flavor, a delicate texture, and they cook in minutes. And if you can find just-picked corn, by all means buy it.

SERVES 4

Baked Peppers with Cream

1 1/2 lb (750 g) red bell peppers (capsicums) (4 or 5)

2 tablespoons minced shallot

6–8 large fresh basil leaves, thinly shredded (2–3 tablespoons), plus whole basil leaves for garnish

3/4 cup (6 fl oz/180 ml) heavy (double) cream

Salt and freshly ground pepper

★ Roast and peel the bell peppers *(see page 121)*. Set aside.

★ Position a rack in the middle of the oven and reduce the temperature to 375°F (190°C). Butter a 1 1/2-qt (1.5-l) shallow baking dish.

★ Scatter half of the shallot and half of the shredded basil over the bottom of the prepared dish. Add the pepper halves, cut side down, arranged in a single layer or slightly overlapping. Scatter the remaining shallot and shredded basil over the peppers. Pour the cream over the peppers, making sure they are all evenly moistened. Season to taste with salt and pepper.

★ Place in the oven and bake uncovered, basting several times with the cream to keep the peppers moist, until the cream thickens and the peppers are tender when pierced with a fork, 30–35 minutes.

★ Garnish with the basil leaves and serve at once.

Cream works wonders with vegetables. Red bell peppers, for example, become rich, tender, and wonderfully sweet when baked in a little cream, making a beautiful side dish for a special meal featuring grilled steak, chops, or fish. You can substitute yellow or orange bell peppers, or prepare a mixture. Don't use green peppers, however, as they lack the necessary sweetness. The ingredients can be prepared well in advance up to the point of assembling everything in the baking dish.

If fresh basil is unavailable, don't use dried as it doesn't have the same flavor; just omit the basil altogether.

SERVES 4

French Carrots

1 lb (500 g) large carrots (6 or 7)

3–4 tablespoons (1½–2 oz/45–60 g) unsalted butter

2 tablespoons sugar

½ teaspoon salt

1 cup (8 fl oz/250 ml) water

1 lemon

4 or 5 fresh mint sprigs

★ Peel the carrots, then slice on the diagonal about ⅛ inch (3 mm) thick. You should have about 3 cups. Put them into a heavy saucepan with the butter, sugar, salt, and water. Place over medium heat and bring to a boil. Reduce the heat to medium-low and boil gently, uncovered, until the liquid is reduced to 1–2 tablespoons syrup, 20–25 minutes; check the carrots occasionally to be sure they are not scorching. Transfer to a serving dish.

★ Using a zester or fine-holed shredder, and holding the lemon over the carrots, shred the zest (yellow part only) from the skin evenly over the carrots *(see page 122)*.

★ Garnish with the mint sprigs and serve at once.

NOTES

Also known as carrots Vichy, variations of this recipe appear in some early American cookbooks. Vichy water, from the French spa of the same name, was supposed to have made the difference in the cooking. But actually any water will do in this glazing process, which slowly cooks the carrots until the liquid reduces to a spoonful or so of syrup. The addition of lemon zest is my contribution to tradition.

SERVES 4

Jasmine Rice with Shredded Zucchini

1 lb (500 g) small zucchini (courgettes)
Salt
¹/₂ cup (4 fl oz/125 ml) coconut milk, stirred well before using
1¹/₄ cups (10 fl oz/310 ml) water
1 teaspoon peeled and grated fresh ginger
1 cup (7 oz/220 g) jasmine rice, rinsed and drained
3 tablespoons unsalted butter
1 tablespoon minced green (spring) onion, including some tender green tops
Freshly grated nutmeg
1 tablespoon fresh lemon juice
1 lemon

★ Trim the zucchini and shred on a medium-holed shredder; you should have about 3¹/₂ cups. In a colander set over a large bowl, layer half of the zucchini. Sprinkle with salt, then top with the remaining zucchini and again sprinkle with salt. Set aside for 25–30 minutes to drain off the bitter juice. Then, pick up the drained zucchini by small handfuls and squeeze out the released juice. Return the zucchini to the colander and rinse under cold running water to wash out the salt. Again, squeeze out the moisture by handfuls, then set aside.

★ In a heavy saucepan, stir together the coconut milk, water, ginger, and ¹/₂ teaspoon salt. Bring to a rapid boil and gradually add the rice. Reduce the heat to very low, cover, and barely simmer until just tender and the water has been absorbed, 15–20 minutes. Remove from the heat and let stand, covered, for an additional 5 minutes. Uncover and carefully fluff the rice with a fork. Re-cover to keep warm until ready to serve.

★ In a sauté pan or frying pan over medium-high heat, melt the butter. Add the zucchini, green onion, and a little nutmeg. Cook, stirring and tossing, until tender but still opaque, 4–5 minutes, adding a little of the lemon juice toward the end of cooking. Adjust the seasonings with more lemon juice or salt.

★ Arrange the rice around the edge of a warmed serving plate, forming a ring. Spoon the zucchini mixture into the center.

★ Using a zester or fine-holed shredder, and holding the lemon over the zucchini mixture, shred the zest (yellow part only) from the skin evenly over the zucchini *(see page 122)*. Serve at once.

Jasmine rice, a long-grain white rice grown in Thailand, has a fragrant and slightly nutty aroma and flavor, a smooth and shiny surface, and a firm body. Paired here with zucchini, it gains a delightful taste by the addition of coconut milk and fresh ginger.

Once you have shredded, salted, and drained the zucchini, you will find the flavor and texture so much improved that you'll want to repeat the method often. Although the steps sound time-consuming, they really aren't, and removing the vegetable's bitterness and emphasizing its crispness merits the extra effort.

SERVES 4

Cranberry-Orange Muffins

1/3 cup (1 1/2 oz/45 g) dried cranberries, coarsely chopped

2 tablespoons plus 1/3 cup (3 oz/90 g) sugar

3 tablespoons boiling water

1 orange

1 3/4 cups (9 oz/280 g) all-purpose (plain) flour

1/2 cup (2 1/2 oz/75 g) yellow cornmeal

2 1/2 teaspoons baking powder

1/2 teaspoon baking soda (bicarbonate of soda)

1/2 teaspoon salt

2 eggs, at room temperature

1 cup (8 fl oz/250 ml) milk, at room temperature

1/3 cup (3 oz/90 g) unsalted butter, melted

★ Position a rack in the middle of an oven and preheat the oven to 400°F (200°C). Butter the cups of one 12-cup or two 6-cup standard-sized muffin tins.

★ In a small bowl, stir together the dried cranberries and the 2 tablespoons sugar. Stir in the boiling water and set aside for 15 minutes to allow the cranberries to absorb the water and soften.

★ Meanwhile, using a zester or fine-holed shredder, and holding the orange over a saucer, shred the zest (orange part only) from the skin (see page 122). You should have about 1 tablespoon. Set aside.

★ In a large bowl, combine the flour, cornmeal, the 1/3 cup (3 oz/90 g) sugar, baking powder, baking soda, and salt. Stir until well blended. Set aside. In another bowl and using a whisk, beat the eggs lightly. Add the milk and melted butter and beat until smooth. Stir in the cranberries and their remaining liquid and the orange zest.

★ Quickly stir the liquid mixture into the flour mixture; do not overmix. Divide the batter evenly among the prepared muffin tin(s), filling each cup about three-fourths full.

★ Bake until risen and the tops are golden, 20–25 minutes. To test for doneness, insert a wooden toothpick in the center of a muffin; it should come out clean. Transfer to a wire rack and let cool in the tin(s) for 2–3 minutes. Remove from the tin(s) and serve warm. The muffins can be stored in an airtight container overnight.

NOTES

Long a breakfast favorite, one of the secrets to making good muffins is to assemble and combine all the ingredients as quickly as possible, with minimal stirring, and then bake immediately. This ensures that the carbon dioxide gas released by the baking powder causes the muffins to rise in the oven rather than dissipating into the air; the minimal stirring prevents overdevelopment of the flour's gluten, which would produce less tender results.

The muffins are best eaten as soon as they cool to warm; but they're also excellent reheated the next day for 5–6 minutes in a 325°F (165°C) oven. (Do not attempt to warm them in a microwave oven, as their texture will toughen.)

The small amount of cornmeal in the batter gives these muffins a crunchy texture. Dried cherries can be substituted for the cranberries, and lemon for the orange. Serve with Lemon Curd or Apricot-Orange Preserves (recipes on page 120), if you like.

MAKES 12

Toasted Walnut Quick Bread

1 cup (4 oz/125 g) coarsely chopped walnuts

1¹/₂ cups (7¹/₂ oz/235 g) all-purpose (plain) flour

1 cup (5 oz/155 g) whole-wheat (wholemeal) flour

1 tablespoon baking powder

1 teaspoon salt

1 orange

1 egg, at room temperature

1 cup (8 fl oz/250 ml) milk, at room temperature

¹/₄ cup (2 fl oz/60 ml) pure maple syrup

3 tablespoons unsalted butter, melted

★ Position a rack in the middle of an oven and preheat the oven to 325°F (165°C). Butter and flour an 8¹/₂-by-4¹/₂-by-2¹/₂-inch (21-by-11-by-6-cm) loaf pan.

★ Spread out the walnuts on a baking sheet. Place in the oven and bake until they begin to change color, 6–8 minutes. Watch carefully so they do not burn. Remove from the oven and set aside to cool. Increase the oven temperature to 350°F (180°C).

★ In a large bowl, combine the all-purpose flour, whole-wheat flour, baking powder, salt, and toasted walnuts; stir together to mix well. Using a zester or fine-holed shredder, and holding the orange over the bowl containing the flour mixture, shred the zest (orange part only) from the skin *(see page 122)*. Stir and toss together the flour mixture and zest until well blended.

★ In another bowl and using a whisk, beat the egg lightly. Add the milk, maple syrup, and melted butter and beat until smooth. Add the milk mixture to the dry ingredients and stir quickly to combine. Pour into the prepared pan and smooth the top.

★ Bake until well risen and golden, 40–45 minutes. To test for doneness, insert a wooden toothpick into the center of the loaf; it should come out clean. Transfer to a wire rack and let cool in the pan for about 3 minutes. Turn out of the pan and leave on the rack, right side up, to cool completely.

★ Cut into slices to serve.

NOTES

Since the introduction of soda bread by the first Irish immigrants, quick breads have been an important part of American baking. The invention of baking powder brought a still greater variety of breads, cakes, and muffins to the country's kitchens. Most quick breads resemble cake as much as bread, and they are at their best eaten right after baking. But dried fruit or nut breads such as this one keep very well for up to 3 days and are excellent for sandwiches or with salads or cold meats. To store, wrap tightly with plastic wrap and keep in a cool place or in the refrigerator.

I believe this bread tastes best the day after it is baked. The walnuts contribute a wonderful texture, and the inclusion of whole-wheat flour adds still more crunch. Try the bread lightly toasted and spread with Lemon Curd or Apricot-Orange Preserves *(recipes on page 120)*.

MAKES 1 LOAF

Spoon Corn Bread

3 cups (24 fl oz/750 ml) milk
Pinch of freshly grated nutmeg
1 teaspoon salt
1 cup (5 oz/155 g) yellow cornmeal
2 tablespoons unsalted butter, cut into small cubes
4 eggs
2 teaspoons baking powder
1/4 cup (1 oz/30 g) freshly grated Parmesan cheese

★ Position a rack in the middle of an oven and preheat the oven to 425°F (220°C). Butter a 1¹/₂-qt (1.5-l) soufflé dish or other deep baking dish.

★ In a large, heavy saucepan over medium heat, add the milk and heat until small bubbles form along the edges of the pan; do not allow it to boil. Remove from the heat and add the nutmeg and salt. Then, while vigorously stirring (preferably with a whisk), slowly add the cornmeal. (The vigorous stirring is necessary to avoid lumping.) Continue to beat until smooth. Return the pan to low heat and, while stirring continuously, add the butter, a few pieces at a time, until melted and mixed in, about 1 minute. Remove from the heat.

★ In a bowl, combine the eggs and baking powder and, using a fork or whisk, beat until light and frothy, 3–4 seconds. Stir the egg mixture into the cornmeal mixture just until blended. Lastly, stir in the Parmesan cheese. Pour into the prepared dish.

★ Bake until puffed and golden, 35–40 minutes. To test for doneness, insert a wooden toothpick into the center; it should come out clean. Serve at once.

NOTES

Also known as spoonbread, spoon corn bread is a great specialty of the American South—a cross between corn bread, pudding, and a soufflé. Dish it out with a spoon, as its name suggests, to accompany family-style main courses. If you like, drizzle each serving with Roasted Red Pepper Sauce (recipe on page 120), thinned with a little chicken stock or water.

In the earliest recipes for spoonbread, the eggs were beaten vigorously to incorporate air to help the spoon-bread rise. After baking powder became popular, most cooks added a little to ensure lightness.

You can use white or yellow corn-meal, although I prefer the flavor and color of the yellow. Imported Parmesan cheese gives the best taste to the mixture. For a little hotness, add 1 or 2 small fresh chile peppers, seeded and chopped, to the batter.

SERVES 4

Cream Scones

2¹/₄ cups (9 oz/280 g) cake (soft-wheat) flour
¹/₄ cup (2 oz/60 g) sugar
¹/₂ teaspoon salt
2 teaspoons baking powder
2 tablespoons unsalted butter, chilled, cut into small cubes
¹/₃ cup (2 oz/60 g) dried currants
1 orange
1 cup (8 fl oz/250 ml) heavy (double) cream, plus cream for brushing tops

★ Position a rack in the middle of an oven and preheat the oven to 400°F (200°C).

★ In a bowl, combine the cake flour, sugar, salt, and baking powder. Stir until well blended. Drop the butter cubes into the flour mixture and, using a pastry blender, 2 knives, a fork, or your fingertips, cut the butter into the dry ingredients until the mixture resembles coarse crumbs. Stir in the currants.

★ Using a fine-holed grater, and holding the grater over a bowl, grate the zest from the skin of the orange (see page 122). Be sure to include all the zest clinging to the grater. Add the 1 cup (8 fl oz/250 ml) cream to the zest and stir to blend. Using a wooden spoon, quickly stir the cream mixture into the flour mixture.

★ Form the soft dough into a ball and transfer to a lightly floured work surface. With floured hands, knead the dough 4 or 5 times, then roll out (or pat out with your hands) into a 9-inch (23-cm) square about ¹/₂ inch (12 mm) thick. Using a sharp knife, cut the square into 3 strips each about 3 inches (7.5 cm) wide. Cut each strip into 5 triangles. Place on an ungreased baking sheet about ¹/₂ inch (12 mm) apart. Brush the tops of the triangles with cream.

★ Bake until golden, 20–25 minutes. Let cool on the baking sheet for 5–6 minutes, then serve warm.

NOTES

An old English teatime favorite, scones came to the United States with the early settlers. Finely grated orange zest flavors this particular version. They are wonderful served warm with Lemon Curd or Apricot-Orange Preserves (recipes on page 120). Leftover scones can be placed on a baking sheet and warmed in a 350°F (180°C) oven until hot, 6–7 minutes. It's best not to reheat scones in a microwave, as they will become tough and lose their crispness.

I find that cake flour—milled from soft winter wheat, which has less gluten—produces a lighter, flakier scone. If you are a novice at pastry making, I'm sure you'll find a pastry blender works wonders in helping you achieve the desired results quickly and easily.

MAKES 15

Ginger Biscuits

2 cups (10 oz/315 g) all-purpose (plain) flour, plus more if needed
1/4 teaspoon salt
1 tablespoon baking powder
1/4 cup (2 oz/60 g) vegetable shortening
2/3 cup (5 fl oz/160 ml) milk
1 tablespoon sugar
1/2 teaspoon peeled and finely grated fresh ginger

★ Position a rack in the middle of an oven and preheat the oven to 450°F (230°C).

★ In a large bowl, combine the flour, salt, and baking powder. Stir until well blended. Add the shortening and, using a pastry blender, 2 knives, a fork, or your fingertips, cut it into the dry ingredients until the mixture resembles coarse crumbs.

★ Measure the milk in a glass measuring cup. Add the sugar and ginger to the milk and stir until the sugar dissolves and the ginger is mixed in. Using a fork, slowly stir the milk mixture into the flour mixture to form a soft but not sticky dough. You may not need all of the milk. The dough should pull away from the sides of the bowl.

★ Gather up the dough and place on a lightly floured work surface. Knead gently 8–10 times, using extra flour as needed to keep the dough from sticking. Roll out, or pat out with your hands, into a rectangle measuring about 6 by 8 inches (15 by 20 cm) and 1/2 inch (12 mm) thick. Dust a plain or fluted biscuit cutter 2 inches (5 cm) in diameter with flour and cut out the biscuits. Press straight down and do not twist the cutter, to ensure evenly shaped, straight-sided biscuits when baked.

★ Transfer the cutouts to an ungreased baking sheet, spacing them about 1 inch (2.5 cm) apart. Gather the dough scraps together and again roll or pat them out 1/2 inch (12 mm) thick. Cut out more biscuits and transfer to the baking sheet.

★ Bake until golden brown, 8–10 minutes. Serve warm.

NOTES

Biscuits are about as American as bread can get, a part of our cooking culture from colonial times. Easily and quickly prepared, they make a fine addition to almost any meal. I have added freshly grated ginger to this particular recipe, but you can leave it out if you wish. You can also substitute butter for the shortening, although shortening does make a flakier biscuit.

Anyone who has never eaten biscuits as they are made in the American South has a treat in store. The secret lies in the flour, which is milled from soft, locally grown winter wheat that rises higher and produces light, crunchy results.

Serve the biscuits with Lemon Curd or Apricot-Orange Preserves *(recipes on page 120)*.

MAKES 12–14

Parmesan Cheese Bread

3³/₄ cups (19 oz/600 g) unbleached bread flour, or as needed
1 tablespoon active dry yeast
2 teaspoons salt
1¹/₃ cups (11 fl oz/330 ml) warm water (110°F/43°C)
¹/₂ cup (2 oz/60 g) freshly grated Parmesan cheese
Extra-virgin olive oil for brushing

★ In the bowl of a heavy-duty stand mixer, combine the 3³/₄ cups (19 oz/600 g) flour, the yeast, and salt. Add the warm water and stir with a wooden spoon until just mixed together. Sprinkle ¹/₄ cup (1 oz/30 g) of the Parmesan cheese over the dough. Fit the mixer with the dough hook and begin mixing and kneading on very low speed. When the mixture pulls away from the sides of the bowl, increase the mixer speed to medium-low and continue to knead until the dough is smooth and elastic, 12–15 minutes, adding more flour if too sticky. Transfer the dough to a floured work surface and knead by hand for 1–2 minutes.

★ Form the dough into a ball, brush it with a little olive oil, and return it to the bowl. Cover with a towel and let rest in a warm, draft-free place until doubled in volume, 1–1¹/₂ hours.

★ Position a rack in the lower part of an oven and preheat the oven to 425°F (220°C). Brush a 9-inch (23-cm) round pan with olive oil. Place the remaining ¹/₄ cup (1 oz/30 g) Parmesan cheese on a plate. Punch down the dough. Return it to the floured work surface and knead a few times. Then, using your palms, roll to form the dough into a log about 12 inches (30 cm) long. Cut the log in half crosswise, then cut each half crosswise into 6 equal pieces. Knead each dough piece a couple of times, roll it between the palms of your hands into a ball, and then roll it in the cheese to coat lightly and evenly, shaking off any excess. As each ball is coated, place it in the prepared pan, resting it against the rim and pressing down slightly to form a 2-inch (5-cm) disk. Arrange 9 balls around the rim and 3 balls in the center. Cover loosely with plastic wrap and let rise again in a warm place until doubled in size, 30–40 minutes.

★ Sprinkle the top with the cheese remaining on the plate. Using a razor blade or sharp knife, cut a slash ¹/₄ inch (6 mm) deep in the top of each ball. Bake for 10 minutes. Reduce the oven temperature to 375°F (190°C) and continue baking until brown and crusty, 20–30 minutes longer. Transfer to a wire rack and let rest in the pan for 1–2 minutes, then remove from the pan; the rolls will come out in a single loaf.

★ Serve the loaf warm, breaking off the rolls at the table. Or let cool, top side up, on the rack.

NOTES

Make this bread for a party, serving it while still warm and breaking off individual rolls at the table. If necessary, you can reheat it in a 300°F (150°C) oven; don't use a microwave oven, which will toughen the bread.

The dough can also be made by hand: Stir together the ingredients in a bowl and then knead the dough on a lightly floured board until smooth and elastic, about 15 minutes.

Use freshly grated Parmesan cheese, preferably imported. You will achieve better results in bread making if you seek out one of the high-quality active dry yeasts, such as Engedura from Holland or SAF from France. Both are available at specialty-food stores.

I use a 9-inch (23-cm) round cake pan with 1¹/₂-inch (4-cm) straight sides for this bread, but any pan of approximate capacity can be used.

MAKES 12 ROLLS

Apricot Bread-and-Butter Custard

6–8 slices Italian or French bread, each $1/2$ inch (12 mm) thick
$1/2$ cup (5 oz/155 g) Apricot-Orange Preserves *(recipe on page 120)*
2–3 tablespoons unsalted butter, at room temperature
1 orange
3 cups (24 fl oz/750 ml) milk
1 cup (8 fl oz/250 ml) heavy (double) cream
$1/2$ cup (4 oz/125 g) granulated sugar
3 whole eggs plus 4 egg yolks
Confectioners' (icing) sugar

★ Position a rack in the middle of an oven and preheat the oven to 325°F (165°C). Butter a shallow 2-qt (2-l) baking dish, preferably oval or rectangular. Have ready a baking pan about 3 inches (7.5 cm) deep that is large enough to accommodate the baking dish. Bring a teakettle full of water to a boil.

★ Arrange 3 or 4 bread slices in the prepared dish; trim as necessary to avoid overlapping. It is not necessary to fill the space completely. Spread the slices evenly with the preserves. Arrange a second layer of bread slices on top. Spread with the butter. Set aside.

★ Grate the zest from the orange *(see page 122)*. In a saucepan over medium heat, combine the milk, cream, and 2 teaspoons of the orange zest. Heat until bubbles form along the edge of the pan; do not boil. Set aside.

★ In a large bowl, combine the granulated sugar, whole eggs, and egg yolks. Using a whisk, beat until well blended. Gradually add the hot milk, stirring continuously with the whisk just until blended.

★ Place the baking dish in the baking pan. Carefully pour the hot custard mixture into the dish so that it flows between the bread and the side of the dish, not over the bread. Pour in only enough custard to reach halfway up the bottom layer of bread. Let stand for a few minutes for the bread to absorb some of the custard. Pour in the rest of the custard. Using a large spatula, press the slices down even with the top of the custard and hold them there for a few seconds to help the bread absorb more. Pour water into the baking pan to reach two-thirds up the sides of the baking dish.

★ Bake until just set, 40–45 minutes. To test, insert a knife into the custard near the center; it should come out clean. Do not overbake, as the custard will separate. Transfer the baking dish to a wire rack to cool slightly. The pudding is best if served warm. Just before serving, sieve confectioners' sugar generously over the top.

NOTES

Bread pudding has long been a favorite in the United States. Lately, however, European-style bread-and-butter custards have been gaining increasing popularity.

An oval Pyrex baking dish measuring $10^1/2$ by 8 by $2^1/4$ inches (26 by 20 by 5.5 cm) works well for this recipe. The key to the success of this pudding is the bread itself. Use a good Italian or French type with a fairly tough crumb that will hold up well in liquid, without getting mushy the way most commercial sandwich-type loaves do.

I prefer to make my own jam from dried apricots *(recipe on page 120)*, because I can control the sugar and produce a more intense, tart apricot flavor. To my taste, the resulting jam contrasts much better with the soft, rich custard. If you wish, add a little more sugar to the jam. Of course, you can also use any brand of high-quality apricot preserves that is not overly sweet.

SERVES 6

Poached Pears and Blueberries

4 cups (32 fl oz/1 l) water

3 cups (24 oz/750 g) sugar

2 lemons

4 ripe but firm pears such as Comice, Bosc, or Bartlett (Williams), preferably with their stems attached

2 cups (8 oz/250 g) blueberries

Whipped Cream Sauce *(recipe on page 120)*

★ In a large saucepan, combine the water, sugar, and the juice of 1 of the lemons. Place over medium-high heat and bring to a boil, stirring to dissolve the sugar. Remove from the heat and set aside.

★ Working from the bottom of each pear, carefully remove the core, cutting no farther than three-fourths of the way toward the stem end. Do not remove the stem. Peel the pears and, if necessary, cut a thin slice off the bottom of each to make them stand upright. Place the pears in the syrup, return the pan to the heat, and quickly bring back to a boil. Lower the heat and simmer until the pears are tender when pierced with a sharp knife, 20–25 minutes. Turn the pears at intervals so they cook evenly, stay moist, and do not turn brown. Using a slotted spoon, transfer the pears to a dish to cool. Reserve 1/2 cup (4 fl oz/125 ml) of the syrup; refrigerate the remaining syrup for another use.

★ In a saucepan, combine the blueberries and the 1/2 cup (4 fl oz/125 ml) reserved poaching syrup. Place over medium heat and bring just to a simmer. Reduce the heat slightly and simmer uncovered until the berries are tender, 10–15 minutes. Set aside to cool.

★ When ready to serve, transfer the pears, stem end up, to individual dessert plates and spoon the blueberries around them. Dribble some of the blueberries over the pears, as well, if you like. Using a zester or fine-holed shredder, and holding the remaining lemon over each pear, shred the zest (yellow part only) from the skin evenly over the top *(see page 122)*.

★ Stir the Whipped Cream Sauce and spoon a little over each pear. Serve the remaining cream sauce in a bowl at the table.

NOTES

Poaching is one of the best ways to prepare pears for a simple and delicious dessert, and with little effort a special presentation can be achieved. Make this in the fall when both pears and blueberries are at their peak, or during the early winter, substituting cranberries if blueberries are not available. Raspberries and blackberries can be used as well.

I have found that Comice pears poach extremely well. Select ones that are ripe but still firm. If using the Bosc variety, you may find them difficult to core while retaining the stem. A tip that may help: Make a small incision in the side of the pear about 1 inch (2.5 cm) below the stem end, carefully inserting the knife into the center of the pear to sever the hard core just above the seed pocket.

SERVES 4

Mixed Berry Shortcake

3–4 cups (12–16 oz/375–500 g) mixed berries such as strawberries, raspberries,
  blueberries, and blackberries in any combination
¼ cup (2 oz/60 g) plus 2 tablespoons granulated sugar
1 cup (4 oz/125 g) cake (soft-wheat) flour
¼ teaspoon salt
1 teaspoon baking powder
1 orange
1½ cups (12 fl oz/375 ml) heavy (double) cream
2 tablespoons sour cream
2 tablespoons confectioners' (icing) sugar
1 teaspoon vanilla extract (essence)

★ Position a rack in the middle of an oven and preheat the oven to 400°F (200°C).

★ Wash the berries and shake dry in a colander. If using strawberries, cut them in halves or quarters. Cut about one-fourth of any other berries in halves. Put all the berries in a bowl and add the ¼ cup (2 oz/60 g) granulated sugar. Toss well. Cover and refrigerate for at least 30–40 minutes or for up to 1½ hours.

★ In a bowl, stir together the cake flour, the 2 tablespoons granulated sugar, salt, and baking powder. Set aside.

★ Using a zester or small fine-holed shredder, and holding the shredder over a bowl, shred the zest (orange part only) from the skin of the orange (see page 122). Add ½ cup (4 fl oz/125 ml) of the cream to the zest, mixing well, and then stir into the flour mixture until it holds together. Gather into a ball and place on a floured work surface. With floured hands, knead a few times until a soft dough forms, then roll out (or pat out with your hands) into a 6-inch (15-cm) square. Cut into 4 pieces, each 3 inches (7.5 cm) square. Place on an ungreased baking sheet. Bake until golden and crisp, 20–25 minutes. Let cool to warm on the baking sheet.

★ In a bowl, combine the remaining 1 cup (8 fl oz/250 ml) cream and the sour cream and, using a whisk or electric or hand beater, beat just until beginning to thicken. Add the confectioners' sugar and vanilla extract and continue to beat until soft folds form. Cover and refrigerate until ready to serve.

★ Split the warm shortcakes in half horizontally and place the bottom halves on individual plates, cut side up. Spoon some of the berries, with their juices, evenly over the bottoms. Place the tops on them, cut sides down. Spoon on more berries and then the whipped cream. Serve at once.

NOTES

The shortcakes in this recipe are actually scones flavored with orange. Quite crunchy, they go well with the berries, their juice, and the whipped cream. Other soft, juicy fruits such as peaches or nectarines can be used; ice cream can be substituted for the whipped cream; and poached pears can be sliced, sandwiched between the shortcake halves, and topped with a rich dark chocolate sauce.

I purposely specify that the orange zest be shredded over a bowl, so that all the flavorful oil released from the skin during the scraping process is captured. For the topping, I find that combining a little sour cream with the heavy cream for whipping produces a better flavor, similar to the Devonshire cream of England or the crème fraîche of France. Reserve a few of the best-looking berries to use whole for topping, if you like.

SERVES 4

Golden Apple Cobbler

For the filling:

1/2 cup (4 oz/125 g) sugar

1 1/2 tablespoons all-purpose (plain) flour

1/4 cup (2 oz/60 g) unsalted butter

3 lb (1.5 kg) Golden Delicious apples, peeled, cored, and thinly sliced

2 tablespoons fresh lemon juice

1 teaspoon vanilla extract (essence)

For the crust:

2 cups (10 oz/315 g) all-purpose (plain) flour

1/4 cup (2 oz/60 g) sugar

2 teaspoons baking powder

1/4 teaspoon salt

2 tablespoons unsalted butter, chilled, cut into small cubes

1/3 cup (3/4 oz/20 g) coarsely chopped crystallized ginger

1 orange

1 cup (8 fl oz/250 ml) heavy (double) cream, plus cream for brushing

Whipped Cream Sauce *(recipe on page 120)*

★ Position a rack in the middle of an oven and preheat to 425°F (220°C). Butter a 1 1/2-qt (1.5-l) pie dish 10 inches (25 cm) in diameter and 2 inches (5 cm) deep.

★ To make the filling, in a bowl, stir together the sugar and flour. In a large sauté pan over medium heat, melt the butter. Stir in the apples, lemon juice, and sugar mixture. Cover partially and cook, stirring, until tender, 15–20 minutes. Stir in the vanilla. Let cool for 15–20 minutes. Transfer to the prepared dish.

★ To make the crust, mix together the flour, sugar, baking powder, and salt in a bowl. Add the butter and, using a pastry blender, 2 knives, or your fingertips, cut in the butter until the mixture resembles coarse crumbs. Stir in the ginger.

★ Grate the zest from the orange into a bowl *(see page 122)*. Be sure to include all the zest clinging to the grater. Stir in the cream. Then, using a fork, stir the cream-zest mixture into the flour mixture, just until it holds together. Gather the dough into a ball. On a floured work surface and with floured hands, knead briefly until soft, then roll out a little larger than the pie dish. Transfer the round to the dish; trim off excess. Cut a small hole in the center for steam to escape. Cut any scraps into fanciful shapes. Brush the top with cream where you wish to decorate, then press the shapes in place. Lightly brush the crust and decorations with cream.

★ Bake for 10 minutes. Reduce the heat to 375°F (190°C) and bake until golden, 20–25 minutes longer. Cool on a wire rack. Serve warm, topped with Whipped Cream Sauce.

NOTES

The flaky crusts characteristic of pie making in our grandmothers' day are sadly becoming a lost art: Only cooks with a natural talent for pastry making continue to turn out those tender, light crusts. But that doesn't mean that delectable pies must become a thing of the past. If you find pastry making too difficult, try preparing other types of "pies" such as this deep-dish cobbler—every bit the equal, I think, of a traditional apple pie.

For this recipe, I use Golden Delicious apples here for their wonderful flavor. Also, their firm texture doesn't break down during cooking, so there's less chance of their juice boiling over in the oven. You can also use Fuji apples, which are sweet and have crisp white flesh. Partially cooking the apples before assembling the cobbler cuts down on the baking time and assures that the apples are thoroughly cooked.

SERVES 6–8

Chocolate-Orange Cheesecake

Graham crackers for 1¹/₂ cups (4¹/₂ oz/140 g) crumbs

2 tablespoons plus ³/₄ cup (6 oz/185 g) sugar

1 tablespoon unsweetened cocoa, plus additional cocoa for dusting top

1 teaspoon ground cinnamon

¹/₄ cup (2 oz/60 g) unsalted butter, melted

8 oz (250 g) bittersweet chocolate, chopped

1 orange

1 lb (500 g) cream cheese, at room temperature

¹/₂ cup (4 fl oz/125 ml) sour cream

5 eggs

★ Position a rack in the middle of an oven and preheat the oven to 350°F (180°C). Cover the outside (bottom and sides) of a 9-inch (23-cm) springform pan with aluminum foil, shiny side out. Butter the inside of the pan generously.

★ Place the graham crackers between 2 sheets of waxed paper and, using a rolling pin, crush to form fine crumbs. Measure out 1¹/₂ cups (4¹/₂ oz/140 g) and place in a bowl. Add the 2 tablespoons sugar, the 1 tablespoon cocoa, and the cinnamon and mix well. Gradually add the melted butter, stirring constantly, until the crumbs are evenly coated. Place in the prepared pan and, using your fingers, press evenly over the bottom and two-thirds up the sides. Refrigerate until ready to fill.

★ Place the chocolate in a heatproof bowl or in the top pan of a double boiler. Set the bowl or pan over (but not touching) 1 inch (2.5 cm) of barely simmering water in a saucepan or the bottom pan of the double boiler. Stir until melted and smooth. Remove the bowl or pan from over the water and set aside.

★ Using a fine-holed grater, grate the zest from the orange (see page 122). Be sure to include all the zest clinging to the grater. Set aside. Place the cream cheese in a bowl. Using an electric mixer set on medium speed, beat until smooth and fluffy and no lumps remain, about 10 minutes. Beat in the sour cream, then beat in the ³/₄ cup (6 oz/185 g) sugar and the orange zest. Add the eggs, one at a time, beating well after each addition. Beat for 1–2 minutes until fully blended.

★ Using a rubber spatula, gently stir in the melted chocolate until blended; do not beat. Continue to stir slowly for 1–2 minutes to dispel as many bubbles as possible. Pour the batter into the prepared pan. Bake until puffed and no longer shiny, about 50 minutes. The center may still look slightly liquid, but it will firm up when chilled. Transfer to a wire rack to cool. When cold, remove the foil, then remove the pan sides. Cover and refrigerate until firm enough to cut easily, 4–5 hours.

★ Just before serving, sieve cocoa generously over the cake.

NOTES

The flavors of chocolate and orange, which complement each other so well, make wonderful additions to a tangy cheesecake. If possible, use a Dutch-process cocoa, which has a smoother flavor than other cocoas.

Several important points will help you achieve a good, smooth, light cheesecake. First, cover the outside of the pan with aluminum foil, shiny side out, to slow down the heat absorption and promote even baking. Next, let the cream cheese soften to room temperature and then beat it until very light and fluffy and free of all lumps; scrape down the sides of the bowl often to make sure you haven't missed any lumps. Third, beat in each egg thoroughly before adding the next one. Finally, slowly stir the batter to dispel as many bubbles as possible before pouring it into the baking pan; this step may take a few minutes.

SERVES 6–8

Lime-Pecan Butter Cookies

2 cups (10 oz/315 g) all-purpose (plain) flour

1/4 cup (1 oz/30 g) cornstarch (cornflour)

1/4 teaspoon salt

3/4 cup (6 oz/185 g) sugar

1 cup (3 1/2 oz/105 g) pecans, coarsely chopped

1 lime

3/4 cup (6 oz/180 g) unsalted butter, cut into cubes

1 egg white

★ Position a rack in the middle of an oven and preheat the oven to 350°F (180°C). Butter 2 baking sheets.

★ In a bowl, sift together the flour, cornstarch, and salt. Set aside.

★ In a food processor fitted with the metal blade or in a blender in two batches, combine 1/4 cup (2 oz/60 g) of the sugar and the pecans. Pulse until finely chopped. Set aside.

★ Using a small fine-holed grater, and holding the grater over a saucer, grate the zest (green part only) from the skin of the lime (see page 122). Be sure to include all the zest clinging to the grater. You should have about 1/2 teaspoon. Cut the lime in half and squeeze the juice into a small bowl. Set the zest and juice aside.

★ In a bowl, combine the remaining 1/2 cup (4 oz/125 g) sugar and the butter. Using a heavy-duty electric mixer set on medium speed, beat until light, about 5 minutes, scraping down the sides of the bowl as needed. Add the egg white, the lime zest, and 2 teaspoons of the lime juice and continue beating until fluffy, another 8–10 minutes, again scraping down the sides of the bowl as needed. Reduce the speed to low and carefully beat in the flour mixture, a little at a time. Add the pecans and beat until well blended.

★ Using a small spoon, scoop up spoonfuls of the dough and, using your hands, form into balls about 1 inch (2.5 cm) in diameter. Place on the prepared baking sheets about 1 inch (2.5 cm) apart. Using a thumb, press down on each ball to flatten it to about 3/8 inch (9 mm) thick, leaving a thumbprint in the dough.

★ Bake until the cookies just begin to color at the edges, 18–20 minutes. Transfer the baking sheets to wire racks to cool for 3–4 minutes, then transfer the cookies to the racks to cool completely. Store in airtight containers for up to 1 week.

NOTES

Light and crunchy, these butter cookies are flavored with just a hint of lime.

For the best results, weigh or measure your ingredients carefully. When using any size measuring cup to measure flour, scoop up the flour with a smaller cup or a scoop and place it loosely in the measuring cup until the cup is full. Then, using the back of a straight-bladed knife or a spatula, evenly scrape off the top. Scooping out the flour with the measuring cup itself would pack it down, giving you too much.

The texture of the cookies also depends on beating enough air into the dough. Start by thoroughly beating together the butter and sugar, scraping down the bowl several times. Then add the egg white and lime juice and beat again until light and fluffy. Do not make the cookies too big: Form balls of dough no more than 1 inch (2.5 cm) in diameter.

MAKES 60–65

Lemon-Almond Butter Cake

1/2 cup (2 oz/60 g) sliced (flaked) almonds

1 3/4 cups (5 1/2 oz/170 g) cake (soft-wheat) flour, sifted before measuring

2 teaspoons baking powder

1/4 teaspoon salt

2 lemons

1/2 cup (4 oz/125 g) unsalted butter, at room temperature

1 cup (8 oz/250 g) sugar

2 eggs, beaten

1/2 cup (4 fl oz/125 ml) milk

Lemon Curd *(recipe on page 120)*

★ Position a rack in the middle of an oven and preheat the oven to 300°F (150°C).

★ Butter an 8-inch (20-cm) round cake pan with 2-inch (5-cm) sides. Cut out a piece of waxed paper to fit the bottom of the pan and slip into place. Butter the paper, then dust the paper and the pan sides with flour. Tap out any excess.

★ Spread the sliced almonds on a baking sheet and bake until they begin to change color, 4–5 minutes. Watch carefully so they do not burn. Set aside to cool. Increase the oven temperature to 350°F (180°C).

★ In a large bowl, sift together the sifted cake flour, baking powder, and salt. Set aside. Using a small fine-holed grater, grate the zest from the lemons *(see page 122)*. Be sure to include all the zest clinging to the grater. Set aside.

★ In a large bowl, combine the butter and sugar. Using an electric mixer set on medium speed, beat until light and creamy, about 5 minutes, scraping down the sides of the bowl 3 or 4 times. Add the eggs, a little at a time, beating thoroughly after each addition, then continue beating until doubled in volume, 4–5 minutes, again scraping down the sides of the bowl 3 or 4 times. Beat in the lemon zest.

★ Using a rubber spatula, carefully fold in the flour mixture, one-third at a time, alternating with the milk. Spoon into the prepared pan, building up the sides higher than the center. Bake until the top is golden, 35–40 minutes. Insert a toothpick into the center; it should come out clean. Remove from the oven and let rest for a couple of minutes. Using a knife, loosen the sides of the cake from the pan and turn out, bottom side up, onto a wire rack. Peel off the paper and let cool completely.

★ Transfer the cake, bottom side up, to a flat plate. Using a long, sharp knife, cut the cake in half horizontally to form 2 layers. Spread a thin layer of the Lemon Curd on the bottom layer. Replace the top layer and spread the remaining curd over the top and sides of the cake. Scatter the toasted almonds over the top and sides.

NOTES

Although simple to bake and assemble, this recipe yields a splendid-looking cake to serve at a special dinner.

The keys to producing a light, finely grained cake are measuring or weighing the ingredients carefully and beating thoroughly to ensure that ample air is incorporated. Beat the butter and sugar until they are very creamy, scraping down the sides of the bowl frequently to ensure a smooth mixture. Add a little of the egg and beat thoroughly to create an emulsion that doesn't separate. Then continue to add the eggs a little at a time, beating thoroughly each time until well mixed with no sign of separation before adding more. Continue beating until the volume doubles. Next, carefully fold (do not beat) in the flour mixture, one-third at a time, alternating with the liquid.

For a different look, increase the sliced almonds to 3/4 cup (3 oz/90 g) and simply scatter the nuts more heavily over the cake to cover the icing.

SERVES 8–10

BASIC RECIPES

Roasted Red Pepper Sauce

1 1/2 lb (750 g) red bell peppers (capsicums)
2 tablespoons extra-virgin olive oil
1 small white Bermuda onion, finely diced
  (3/4 cup/4 oz/125 g)
1/2 cup (4 fl oz/125 ml) chicken stock or water
1/4 teaspoon salt
Pinch of red pepper flakes
1 teaspoon minced fresh marjoram

Roast and peel the bell peppers as directed *(see page 121)*. Chop coarsely. ★ In a frying pan over low heat, warm the oil. Add the onion and sauté until translucent, about 5 minutes. Add the peppers, stock or water, salt, pepper flakes, and marjoram; cover and simmer until the onion and peppers are tender, about 20 minutes.★ Transfer to a food processor fitted with the metal blade or to a blender. Process to a coarse purée. Return to the pan and reheat gently to serving temperature. Taste and adjust the seasonings. ★ Can be stored tightly covered in the refrigerator for 2–3 days.

MAKES ABOUT 1 1/2 CUPS (12 FL OZ/375 ML)

Apricot-Orange Preserves

8 oz (250 g) dried apricots, picked over and rinsed
1 small orange
1 1/4 cups (10 fl oz/310 ml) water
1/3 cup (3 oz/90 g) sugar

Place the apricots in a saucepan. Using a zester or fine-holed shredder, shred the zest from the orange *(see page 122)* over the apricots. Add the water and bring to a boil. Reduce the heat to low and simmer, uncovered, until the apricots are soft and most of the water has been absorbed, about 20 minutes. Transfer to a food processor fitted with the metal blade or to a blender; process to a coarse purée. ★ Return the purée to the saucepan and add the sugar. Place over low heat and stir until the sugar dissolves, 2–3 minutes. Add a little water if too stiff. Remove from the heat and let cool. Can be stored tightly covered in the refrigerator for 2–3 weeks.

MAKES ABOUT 1 1/2 CUPS (15 OZ/470 G)

Lemon Curd

2 or 3 lemons
1/2 cup (4 oz/125 g) sugar
3 eggs
1/2 cup (4 oz/125 g) unsalted butter, cut into small cubes

Using a fine-holed grater, grate the zest from 1 lemon *(see page 122)*. Cut the lemons in half and squeeze enough juice to measure 1/3 cup (3 fl oz/80 ml). ★ In a heavy saucepan, combine the lemon juice and zest, sugar, and eggs. Whisk until well blended. Place over medium-low heat. While stirring constantly, add the butter, a few cubes at a time, letting the cubes melt before adding more and scraping the bottom of the pan each time. Cook slowly, stirring continuously, until thickened, 10–15 minutes. The curd should be smooth and free of lumps. ★ Transfer to a bowl and cover with plastic wrap, pressing the wrap directly onto the surface of the curd. Refrigerate or set aside to cool. ★ Can be stored tightly covered in the refrigerator for up to 1 week.

MAKES ABOUT 1 1/2 CUPS (12 FL OZ/375 ML)

Whipped Cream Sauce

Ice cubes
3 egg yolks
1/4 cup (1 oz/30 g) confectioners' (icing) sugar
1 tablespoon Grand Marnier or 2 teaspoons vanilla extract
1 cup (8 fl oz/250 ml) heavy (double) cream

Have ready a pan of ice, mixed with a little water. ★ In a heatproof bowl, combine the egg yolks, sugar, and Grand Marnier or vanilla extract. Whisk until frothy. Place the bowl over (but not touching) barely simmering water in a saucepan. Using a whisk or electric mixer, beat until light colored and thickened, 5–6 minutes. Do not beat too long, and do not allow the yolks to get too hot or they will curdle. Nest the bowl in the ice and continue beating until cold. The mixture will become quite thick. Set aside. ★ In another bowl, whip the cream until thick, soft folds form. Stir the cream into the cooled egg yolk mixture just until blended and smooth. Serve immediately, or cover and refrigerate for up to several hours, stirring again just before serving. ★ Any leftover sauce can be covered and refrigerated for up to 24 hours and then stirred well before serving.

MAKES ABOUT 2 1/2 CUPS (20 FL OZ/625 ML)

TECHNIQUES

Roasting Bell Peppers

Bell peppers (capsicums)—especially the ripened red, yellow, and orange varieties—have a natural sweetness and a juicy texture that are heightened by roasting. While many different methods exist for roasting peppers, the one shown here streamlines the process by halving, stemming, and seeding them first, leaving only the peeling of the blackened skins after the peppers have cooled.

Using a Food Mill

A food mill is a mechanical sieve that creates an even-textured purée. Although cranked by hand, in some cases it can do a job faster than the time it would take to purée in a food processor and then sieve that purée. Cooked vegetables or fruits are pushed against the holes in the bottom of the mill by a paddle fitted with a tension spring; the solids are forced through the holes, which hold back any seeds, skins, and fibers. Imported models usually come with medium and fine disks.

1 Halving, Stemming, and Seeding

Preheat a broiler (griller) or an oven to 500°F (260°C). Using a small, sharp knife, cut each pepper in half length-wise. Cut out the stem, seeds, and white ribs from each half.

1 Ladling in the Ingredients

Set the food mill securely atop a large bowl. Ladle in the food to be puréed—here, a cooked soup—making sure to include any liquids along with the solids.

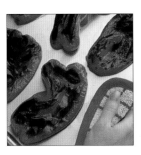

2 Roasting the Peppers

Lay the pepper halves, cut sides down, on a baking sheet. Place under the broiler or in the oven. Broil (grill) or roast until the skins blister and blacken.

2 Turning the Mill

Steadying the mill with one hand, turn its handle clockwise to force the ingredients through the disk. From time to time, turn the handle counter-clockwise to dislodge fibrous material from the disk's surface.

3 Peeling the Peppers

Remove from the oven and cover with aluminum foil. Let steam until cool enough to handle, 10–15 minutes. Then, using your fingers or a knife, peel off the skins.

3 Finishing the Purée

Continue ladling ingredients and turning the mill until the purée is complete. Remove the mill and stir the purée to give it an even consistency, returning it to a pan if necessary for gentle reheating.

Sectioning Citrus Fruit

When citrus fruit is used as a garnish or in a dessert or salad, recipes frequently call for it to be sectioned, or segmented—that is, cut free from its pith and membranes, the better to enjoy the fruit's flavor, texture, and color. The only tool needed to perform this task is a good, sharp knife. Bear in mind that the process yields the most attractive results when you start with citrus fruits that have few if any seeds; use the tip of a small, sharp knife to remove any visible seeds after sectioning.

Cutting Citrus Zest

Zest, the thin, brightly colored, outermost layer of a citrus fruit's peel, contains most of the peel's aromatic essential oils—which provide a lively source of flavor for savory and sweet dishes alike. Depending upon how the zest will be combined with other ingredients, how intense a citrus flavor is desired, and what decorative effects are called for, the zest may be removed in one of several different ways, shown below. Whichever way you use, take care to remove the colored zest only; the white, spongy pith beneath it is bitter and, if used, can mar the flavor of the dish.

1 Trimming the Fruit

To enable the citrus fruit—here, a grapefruit—to be steadied on the work surface, use a sharp, thin-bladed knife to cut a thick slice off its bottom and top, exposing the fruit beneath the peel.

Grating Zest

For very fine particles of citrus zest, lightly rub the fruit against the small rasps of a hand-held grater, taking care not to grate away any of the bitter white pith beneath the zest.

2 Cutting Off the Peel

Steadying the fruit upright on the work surface, thickly slice off the peel in strips, cutting off the white pith and membrane with it to reveal the fruit sections.

Shredding Zest

Using a simple tool known as a zester, draw its sharp-edged holes across the fruit's skin to remove the zest in thin shreds. Alternatively, use a fine-holed shredder, which has small indented slots to cut shreds.

3 Cutting Out the Sections

Hold the peeled fruit in one hand over a bowl to catch the juices. Using the same knife, carefully cut on each side of the membrane to free each section, letting the sections drop into the bowl.

Cutting Wide Strips

Holding the edge of a paring knife or vegetable peeler almost parallel to the fruit's skin, carefully cut off the zest in strips, taking care not to remove any white pith with it.

Preparing Fresh Shrimp

Raw shrimp (prawns) are usually sold with the heads already removed but with their shells still on. Most recipes call for peeling shrimp before cooking. And their thin, veinlike intestinal tracts are often removed—principally for the sake of appearance but also to remove a hint of bitterness. After deveining, larger shrimp may be butterflied to help them cook more quickly and evenly. To freshen shrimp before cooking, soak it in salted water for 10–15 minutes, then rinse well in fresh water.

Peeling and Seeding Tomatoes

Tomatoes are one of the great pleasures of the table—especially at the height of summer, when you should seek out the best sun-ripened tomatoes you can find. At other times of year, plum tomatoes, sometimes called Roma or egg tomatoes, are likely to have the best flavor and texture. Often when tomatoes are made into sauces or combined with other ingredients, recipes call for removing their skins and seeds, neither of which contributes much to the prized flavor or texture of the vegetable-fruit.

1 Peeling

Using your thumbs, split open the shrimp's thin shell along the concave side, between the two rows of legs. Peel away the shell. If the recipe calls for it, leave the last shell segment with tail fin intact and attached to the meat.

1 Loosening the Skin

Cut out the core from the stem end of each tomato. Cut a shallow X in the skin at the tomato's base. Gently submerge each tomato in boiling water for 20–30 seconds. Using a slotted spoon, gently remove each tomato and submerge in a bowl of cold water.

2 Deveining

Using a small, sharp knife, carefully make a shallow slit along the shrimp's back, deep enough to expose the long, usually dark, veinlike intestinal tract. With the tip of the knife or your fingers, lift up and pull out the vein.

2 Peeling the Tomato

Starting at the X, peel the skin from the tomato, using your fingertips and, if necessary, the knife blade.

3 Butterflying

To butterfly the shrimp, continue slitting down into the meat just far enough so that, with your fingertips, you can open it out and flatten it easily into two equal-sized lobes. Take care not to cut completely through the shrimp.

3 Seeding the Tomato

Cut the tomato in half crosswise. Holding each half over a bowl, squeeze gently to force out the seed sacs.

Boning and Skinning Chicken

These days so many people buy chicken breasts already skinned and boned at the market that they might not stop to realize the economy that comes with buying whole breasts and taking a few minutes to do the skinning and boning themselves. You can save the bones and any other trimmings to make a simple stock, simmering them with some onion, celery, carrot, parsley, and a bay leaf. For healthier results, make sure to pull or cut off any yellow fat adhering to the surface or edges of the breast or to any trimmings you might use.

1 Removing the Breastbone

Hold the chicken breast skin-side down. Using a knife, slit the thin membrane covering the breastbone along its center. Grasp the breast firmly at each end and flex it upward to pop out the breastbone. Using the knife, pull out the bone.

4 Boning a Breast Half

Starting along the rib side, insert the knife between the bones and meat. Pressing the knife edge gently against the bones, gradually cut the bones away from the meat. Neatly trim the edges of the breast.

2 Cutting the Whole Breast in Half

Place the breast skin-side down on a cutting board. Cut along the center of the breast to separate the two breast halves.

5 Flattening a Breast Half

If a recipe calls for flattening a breast half to help it cook more evenly, place it between 2 sheets of plastic wrap. Using a rolling pin, flatten it to a uniform thickness.

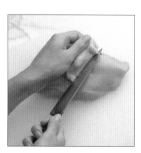

3 Skinning a Half Breast

Place the breast half, skin-side up, on a cutting board. Steady the breast meat with the side of a sturdy knife blade or with your hand; with the other hand, firmly grasp the skin and strip it away from the meat.

INDEX

French carrots 90
fresh chicken sausages with sweet onions and
   grapes 43

G

garden greens and citrus salad 28
ginger biscuits 102
grapefruit
   garden greens and citrus salad 28
green beans
   and corn, circa 1935 87
   broiled shrimp and spinach salad 20
   easy vegetable soup 19

J

jasmine rice with shredded zucchini 93

L

lamb stew with raisins 56
leeks
   in tomato sauce 82
   lamb stew with raisins 56
   tomato-leek soup with dill 16
lemon-almond butter cake 119
lemon curd 120
lime-pecan butter cookies 116

M

macaroni and cheese with broccoli 81
meat
   braised brisket of beef with port wine 48
   corned beef and vegetables 53
   corned beef hash with poached eggs 61
   lamb stew with raisins 56
   meat loaf with red pepper sauce 58
   sautéed pork tenderloin with gingered apples 54
   veal paprika 51
mixed berry shortcake 110
muffins, cranberry-orange 94

O

oranges
   apricot-orange preserves 120
   chocolate-orange cheesecake 115
   cranberry-orange muffins 94
   garden greens and citrus salad 28
   sautéed chicken breasts with ginger-orange
      glaze 37

P

Parmesan cheese bread 105
pears, poached, and blueberries 109
peas, purée of minted green 84
pecan-lime butter cookies 116
peppers
   asparagus mimosa salad 25
   baked, with cream 89
   corn and red pepper salad 31
   preparing and roasting 124
   roasted red pepper sauce 120
   roasted red pepper soup 12
pork
   meat loaf with red pepper sauce 58
   tenderloin with gingered apples, sautéed 54
pot-roasted chicken with onions and potatoes 47
poultry. *See* chicken
preserves, apricot-orange 120
purée of minted green peas 84

Q

quick bread, toasted walnut 96

R

rice
   curried chicken breasts with basmati rice 44
   jasmine rice with shredded zucchini 93
   Spanish rice with shrimp 65
roasted red pepper sauce 120
roasted red pepper soup 12

S

salads
   asparagus mimosa 25
   broiled shrimp and spinach 20
   Caesar 33
   chicken, with apple and walnuts 26
   corn and red pepper 31
   garden greens and citrus 28
   tropical, with lime dressing 23
salmon steaks with cucumbers, poached 66
sauces
   roasted red pepper 120
   whipped cream 120
sausages, fresh chicken, with sweet onions
     and grapes 43
scallops with spinach, sautéed 77

First published in 1995 by
Weldon Owen Inc.
814 Montgomery Street
San Francisco, CA 94133

In collaboration with Williams-Sonoma
3250 Van Ness, San Francisco, CA 94109

The Chuck Williams Collection
Conceived and produced by Weldon Owen Inc.

WILLIAMS-SONOMA
Founder & Vice-Chairman: Chuck Williams

WELDON OWEN INC.
Chief Executive Officer: John Owen
President: Terry Newell
Chief Operating Officer: Larry Partington
VP International Sales: Stuart Laurence
Creative Director: Gaye Allen
Associate Creative Director: Leslie Harrington
Sales Manager: Emily Jahn
Consulting Editor: Laurie Wertz
Assistant Editor: Donita Boles
Art Director: Nicky Collings
Jacket Design: Kari Ontko, India Ink
Production: Chris Hemesath, Teri Bell
Digital Production: Lorna Strutt
Cover Photography: Marshall Gordon
Cover Food Stylist: Diane Scott Gsell

Original design by John Bull, recipe photography by
Allan Rosenberg, and additional photography by Allen V.
Lott. Recipe prop styling by Sandra Griswold and food
styling by Mara Barot. Weldon Owen would like to thank
Carrie Bradley, Kimberly Chun, Juli Vendzules, and Libby
Temple for their assistance and support.

For information about special discounts for bulk purchases,
please contact Weldon Owen Inc. at info@weldonowen.com
or (415) 291-0100.

This edition first published in 2003.
10 9 8 7 6 5 4 3 2

Library of Congress Cataloging-in-Publication Data is available.

ISBN 1 740895 22 3

Printed in China by Midas Printing Limited.

A Note on Weights & Measures:
All recipes include customary U.S. and metric measurements.
Metric conversions are based on a standard developed for these
books and have been rounded off. Actual weights may vary.